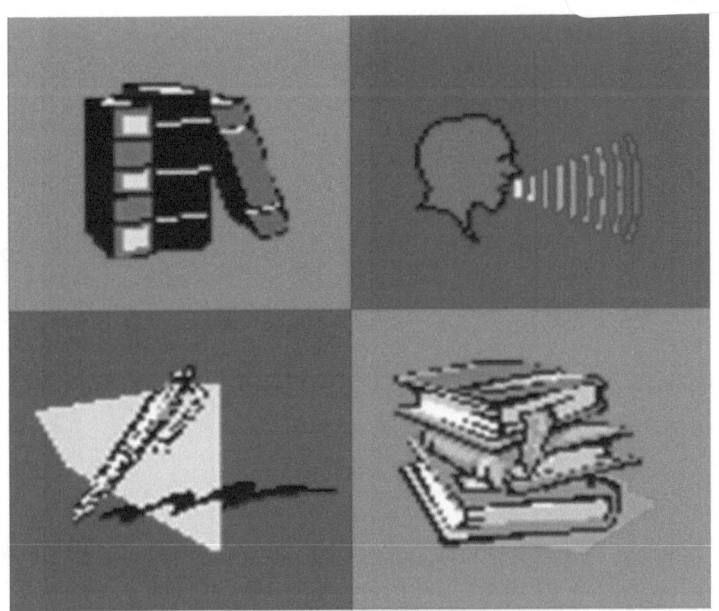

Sybrina's Phrase Thesaurus
Volume 3
Physical Attributes

By Sybrina Durant

Sybrina's Phrase Thesaurus Book – Physical Attributes

©1999 & 2013

Volume 1 - Moving Parts – Part 2 - Print ISBN # ISBN-13: 978-1481928182 & ISBN-10: 148192818X

Volume 2 - Moving Parts – Part 1 - Print ISBN # ISBN-13: 978-1480083189 & ISBN-10: 1480083186

Volume 3 - Physical Attributes – Print ISBN # ISBN-13: 978-1481983051 & ISBN-10: 1481983059

Volume 4 - Earth Views – Print ISBN # ISBN-13: 978-1481983136 & ISBN-10: 148198313X

Other ISBN #'s for Sybrina's Phrase Thesaurus
Ebook - 978-0-9729372-0-7

Contact Sybrina@sybrina.com

Improve your writing skills...Increase your command of the English language with Sybrina's Phrase Thesaurus. If you use a dictionary or thesaurus, you'll love this writer's aid. Tens of thousands of creative phrases...Hundreds of categories to choose from. Excellent writers aid and fun to read, too!

Have you ever hit a brick wall with your writing? Can't always get the creative juices flowing when you need them? Sybrina's Phrase Thesaurus can help you! Wish you had a better way with words? Is English a new language for you? Sybrina's Phrase Thesaurus can help you!

Sybrina's Phrase Thesaurus is a reference tool for anyone with a need to compose unique, descriptive phrases. It's a great tool for creative writers of any genre including students, people just learning English, people wanting to improve their communication skills, artistic professionals like photographers, videographers, models, actors and many others.

Anyone who enjoys reading unique descriptive phrases will love Sybrina's Phrase Thesaurus because it is packed full of descriptive phrases on every subject ...from descriptions of the body, and how it looks, moves and interacts ...to word pictures describing of all types of landscapes, waterscapes and skyscapes.

Just read the phrases and use what you want just as they're written or better yet, read all the suggested phrases in a particular category for inspiration to conquer your writer's block!

Here's how to use it. All of the categories are coded. Just use the index at the back of the book to browse the different categories. Find one you are interested in and use the code to go directly to the group of phrases for that category.

Sybrina's Phrase Thesaurus was first offered for sale, in 1993, in pdf format with a hyperlinked table of contents. The tool is still available at PhraseThesaurus.com. The book has been available, in its entirety, as an Ebook since 2009. The massive size of the book, well over 800 pages, made it financially impossible to offer it in print until the print-on-demand industry became easily available to independent authors and publishers. In order to keep the price of the books in print lower, the book has been split into 4 smaller sections.

The books are sub-titled and described as follows:

Volume 1 - MOVING PARTS – Part 1 - This book encompasses the top half of the body, describing how it moves and functions. Part 1 covers the everything to do with the head, including voluntary and involuntary actions such as listening, blushing breathing, winking, coughing, singing and much more.

Volume 2 - MOVING PARTS – Part 2 - This book encompasses all of the lower body below the neck, describing how it moves and functions. Part 2 covers topics such as shrugging shoulders, reaching out to touch someone, heart beats, shivering, aching bones, stomach churning, hand gestures, posing, sitting, walking, running and much more. The Body In Motion section includes jumping, skipping, turning, sitting down and getting up, bending, stretching, squirming, falling and body in repose. The Daily Activities section includes creative ways to describe eating meals, driving cars, using a telephone, changing clothes and more. The Figures (or Expressions) Of Speech section includes ideas for writing smooth flowing conversations. Much more than just "He said, She said". Finally the Emotions section contains descriptions of emotions. Joy, anger, fear, sadness and many more.

Volume 3 - PHYSICAL ATTRIBUTES – This book encompasses all of the body describing how different parts of the human body look, from head to toe. This book covers topics such as facial shapes and expressions, age and youth. There are descriptions for bald heads and different kinds of hair styles and colors. There are descriptions for skin colors and textures and all kinds of ways to describe eyes, ears, noses and mouths. The rest of the body is described in great detail as well.

Volume 4 - EARTH VIEWS - This book consists of Landscapes (plains, hills, mountains, valleys), Waterscapes (waterfalls, streams, rivers, ponds) and Skyscapes (morning, sunny, cloudy, rain, space, stars) and much more. There is also a section for COLORS with descriptions for all the colors in the rainbow plus other things like metals, shiney, light, dark, day and night.

Enjoy them all!

VOLUME 3 - PHYSICAL ATTRIBUTES

HD
HEAD

HD1 HEAD 1

HD2 HEAD 2 (SHAPES)

1. like a bear's head
2. a round skull
3. long narrow head

HD3 HEAD 3 (LOCATION

1. High-held head
2. top of her head
3. the angle of his head
4. head thrust forward
5. through his head
6. heaviness in his head
7. behind his head
8. in his head
9. the tip of his head

HD4 HEAD 4 (OTHER)

1. a cool head
2. tense nod of consent
3. head ringing like a Chinese gong
4. head ached violently
5. bald head
6. his ringing head
7. head was dizzy and queer swimming head
8. head unbowed

9.   head was uncovered
10.   lightheaded

FA
FACE

FA1 FACE 1

FA2 FACE 2 (SHAPES)

1.   pinched face
2.   heart-shaped face
3.   fat face
4.   thin, intense face
5.   a long, narrow brown face, deeply seamed face
6.   beefy face
7.   a quiet, oval face
8.   dark and rather delicate
9.   broad-carved face
10.   thin face
11.   a flat moon-face
12.   face was coffin-shaped and elegant
13.   a long, drooping mustached face
14.   a quiet oval face, dark, and rather delicate
15.   long face
16.   he looked something like a hawk with mumps
17.   her oval face was daintily pointed
18.   three-cornered face
19.   her face was a perfect oval
20.   the face was long and bony. . .Dutch or Nordic at least
21.   dark eyes framing a handsome square face
22.   the planes of his face were angular
23.   oval face
24.   her facial bones were delicately carved
25.   hawkish face

26.   plump-faced

FA3 FACE 3 (PROFILES)

1.   Well-defined profile
2.   his profile was sharp and confident
3.   his profile, dark against the moonlight
4.   strong-profiled
5.   the clear-cut lines of his profile
6.   the clean purity of her profile
7.   his profile was strong and rigid
8.   his profile was rugged and somber

FA4 FACE 4 (EXPRESSIONS - POSITIVE)

1.   distinguished face
2.   his face was compassionate
3.   face was quite jolly
4.   he had a pale gold, sensitive face
5.   her face showed a delicate dimension of sensitivity
6.   not unkind face
7.   expectant face
8.   a subtle look of amusement
9.   he had that kind of face, that kind of sincerity
10.   a composed look
11.   a cheerful look
12.   schooled face
13.   well-used face
14.   wondering face
15.   his face serious, dedicated
16.   her face was pink with eagerness
17.   placid face
18.   expressive face
19.   a winning expression
20.   a look of enthrallment

21.   expression of innocent childish implorement
22.   expression was hungry and lustful
23.   an expression of rapt attention on his face
24.   her wise-family-friend look
25.   an oblique, quick, half-shy look
26.   a look that was compassionate, troubled and still
27.   complete surprise on his face
28.   face wore a kindly grin
29.   he was handsome with dark eyes and a secret expression
30.   her face was pale, but proud
31.   a new contentment on his face
32.   a shadow of relief on his face
33.   an expression of awe
34.   his expression was that of complete unconcern
35.   a look of implacable determination on his face

FA5 FACE 5 (EXPRESSIONS - NONE)

1.   his expressionless face
2.   expression wiped smooth and blank
3.   implacable expression
4.   his face was thunderous
5.   face was carefully controlled
6.   without a flicker of emotion on her face
7.   expression was a mask of stone
8.   set face
9.   granite-like face
10.   arrested expression
11.   his face was totally devoid of any sign of recognition
12.   his face was stony
13.   with no expression on his face
14.   unresponsive face
15.   his face was granite
16.   mask-like face
17.   entirely neutral expression

18. unreadable expression
19. his mask was cold as a funeral
20. with no expression on his face
21. unreadable features
22. his face was granite, like his eyes
23. face was graven, without expression
24. a set expression on his face
25. face was frozen in calm
26. his face was as still as stone
27. very placid face
28. stony mask of his face
29. her face was inscrutable

FA6 FACE 6 (EXPRESSIONS - NEGATIVE)

1. her face was bleak with sorrow
2. an angry frown
3. fleeting from affronted frown
4. a mask of uncertainty
5. tight expression
6. dark, angry expression
7. frowning in concentration
8. a plump cheery face
9. a flash of anger in her face
10. look of triumph on his face
11. face creased with concern
12. a series of agonized faces
13. determined, eager face
14. his expression was like someone who had been struck in the face
15. glum-faced
16. a bright look of eagerness mixed with a strong stamp of arrogance
17. a coarse, insolent looking man

18. his face had the withered look of an empty balloon
19. an oblique, quick, half-shy look
20. a startled-fawn expression
21. his dark, hawkish face seemed never to have known a smile
22. an expression of awe
23. an "aw, shucks" look on his face
24. horrified expression of disapproval
25. a look of disbelief, rage and frustration
26. her expression was pained, as though she'd been wounded
27. her look was little wary, a little haunted
28. her face, hard, cruel, and pitiless
29. a prim and forbidding expression
30. expression was grim
31. a look of enthrallment
32. tense lines on her face
33. vicious expression
34. face was a glowering mask of rage
35. expression was hungry and lustful
36. his expression was that of complete unconcern
37. a worried look
38. a tense look
39. an inexplicable look of withdrawal
40. an intense but secret expression
41. familiar mask
42. a florid, self-satisfied face
43. disgusted look
44. expression was one of pained tolerance
45. a faintly surprised look
46. a look of fear
47. anxious look on his face
48. he looked wretched
49. stern-faced
50. sullen expression
51. taut features
52. twisted features
53. her face was austere

54. hard-faced
55. smug expression
56. face was naked with anguish
57. silent sadness of his face
58. anxious look on his face
59. a sardonic expression
60. face taut with anger
61. his handsome face was reserved
62. face was stone hard
63. smug expression
64. he had a stubborn, arrogant face
65. his troubled face was like a graveled parking lot
66. a look of sadness
67. closed expression
68. odd soberness on his face
69. the most unwholesome dreamy look
70. a befuddled expression
71. a positively fawning expression
72. her face a mask of fear
73. his expression was one of mute wretchedness
74. fragile composure
75. his expression was tight with strain
76. complete surprise on his face
77. grim purpose in every line of her face
78. shrewd face
79. blackest of scowls
80. quiet shifty look
81. sullen wounded mask
82. with a deceptive look of fragility
83. an expression of awe
84. face blankly alert like a bodyguard's
85. a blind look about her
86. a practiced, half-genial scowl
87. her expression was fierce
88. a look of embarrassingly open adoration
89. face was twisted in disgust

90.   a look of sudden wild misery
91.   an expression of terrifying malignancy on his face
92.   expression was thunderous
93.   a fiery angry look that was unfamiliar
94.   a shade of defiance on his face
95.   face was drawn
96.   his face was a devil's mask of open, insane rage
97.   his face was hard and very white
98.   her stricken expression

FA7 FACE 7 (AESTHETICS - POSITIVE)

1.   handsome face
2.   extremely handsome face
3.   distinguished face
4.   pretty in an elfin way expression
5.   gave the impression of confident masculinity
6.   a face devoid of any blemish or bump that would bar his being called handsome
7.   his arresting face
8.   a chiseled face
9.   he was handsome with dark eyes and a secret expression
10.   The man was exquisite. There was no other word for it.
11.   an American Gothic face
12.   his handsome face was kindled with a sort of passionate beauty
13.   dark eyes framing a handsome square face
14.   his features were so perfect, so symmetrical
15.   that any more delicacy would have made him too beautiful for a man
16.   with a rich, fawnlike beauty
17.   his features were as handsomely sculpted as her own
18.   her face was full of strength
19.   his strong features held a certain sensuality
20.   her prettiness was utterly commonplace

21. a kind of durably boyish face
22. like a face painted on a banner
23. he had an alert, weakly handsome face
24. heavy boned and rakishly good looking
25. face was coffin-shaped and elegant
26. her facial bones were delicately carved
27. her face was pale, but proud
28. arresting good looks
29. a sensuous face, direct and challenging
30. well-defined profile
31. pale and beautiful face
32. there was both delicacy and strength in her face
33. her oval face was daintily pointed
34. boldly handsome face
35. her patrician features
36. her face was arresting, irregular
37. refined looking face
38. a delicate face
39. elegant in looks
40. sweet-faced
41. a quiet, oval face, dark and rather delicate
42. classically handsome features
43. face was fine
44. his hawk-like features arresting and elegant
45. he had a face like a benediction
46. abstract beauty
47. lavishly attractive
48. she was attractive, special, sure of her power to please
49. her uniqueness was alluring
50. looked the part of a pampered matron commonly displayed in society magazines
51. an arrogantly handsome woman of undisclosed age
52. her cool porcelain good looks
53. in repose, she was almost ugly, but in animation, she was beautiful
54. pleasant-faced

55.	her face was well modeled and feminine
56.	a vividly beautiful woman
57.	an incredibly desirable woman
58.	she was, simply put, a startlingly attractive woman
59.	an aura of untouchable glory about her
60.	happy-faced
61.	face retaining traces of beauty
62.	kind face
63.	deep-lined, still handsome face
64.	there was an inherent strength in his face
65.	his ruggedly handsome face was vaguely familiar
66.	her beauty was so unearthly it was frightening
67.	wholesome good looks
68.	heavy-boned and rakishly good looking
69.	she was beautiful with the bounteous magnificence of an earth mother
70.	his classically handsome features
71.	an identical remake of her mother
72.	a lovely, skillfully made, richly evocative woman
73.	a beautiful china-skinned blond girl
74.	her face was simply a frame for her eyes

FA8 FACE 8 (AESTHETICS - NEGATIVE)

1.	careworn face
2.	homely face
3.	foxy face
4.	coarse,
5.	heavily veined face
6.	her face was arresting, irregular
7.	he was her flour-faced husband
8.	a face like a woodchuck
9.	a bad animated caricature of a face
10.	the face of a bad night
11.	a haughty man with craggy features
12.	good looks had been bred out

13. there was something terribly plastic looking about her
14. arrogant, sallow features
15. a chillingly evil face
16. he had an alert, weakly handsome face
17. a gangly youth with a blotchy face
18. a slightly blurred face, the kind you can't remember
19. a drinker's veined face
20. he looked something like a hawk with mumps
21. harsh features
22. her face was austere
23. homely face
24. dark, hawkish face
25. face was work-hardened
26. tense lines on her face
27. a long raw scratch on his face
28. the angles of his face harsh in the light

FA9 FACE 9 (LOCATIONS)

1. upturned face
2. on her face
3. her upturned face
4. her face white beneath her tan
5. face to face
6. across the side of his serious face
7. in his face
8. out of his face
9. his whole face
10. down her face

FA10 FACE 10 (SHOWING AGE - OLD)

1. deeply etched face
2. face had become haggard and old
3. eyes were sunk in the pallid hollow of his face

4. sun-whacked face
5. a long, narrow brown face, deeply seamed
6. the face of a man in the last year or so of his life
7. an old man's face, seamed and lined
8. plain and elderly
9. engraved with bitter lines
10. a badly preserved forty-nine
11. he had a well-used face
12. craggy face
13. face was old
14. her face a network of tiny lines
15. craggy face
16. sun-toughened face
17. a prim-looking woman in her late fifties
18. heavy lined face

FA11 FACE 11 (SHOWING AGE - YOUNG)

1. hairless face
2. girlish prettiness
3. small puckered face
4. boyish face
5. ageless face
6. face was smooth
7. tight face
8. face of a child
9. face retaining traces of youth
10. immature face
11. face felt tight and tangy
12. face was like seamed marble

FA12 FACE 12 (FACIAL COLOR)

1. White-faced

2. color had drained from her face making her hair darker than ever
3. face drained of color
4. deathly pallor his face was puce in the flickering light
5. her face white and strained
6. his face red from the cold
7. a long, narrow brown face, deeply seamed
8. arrogant, sallow features
9. her face was pink with eagerness
10. her face was clear, almost bloodless
11. he had a pale gold, sensitive face
12. her cool porcelain good looks
13. a gangly youth with a blotchy face
14. his face was bronzed by wind and sun
15. tanned face
16. he had the pallor of desk work
17. a grayish pallor under his skin
18. a quiet oval face, dark, and rather delicate
19. a pale-complexioned face
20. burning face
21. pallid face
22. face was pale
23. her face white beneath her tan
24. her ivory face had a musk-rose flush
25. her complexion was white and illusive pink
26. ashen face
27. pale and beautiful face
28. a florid face
29. dark, hawkish face
30. drained face
31. sun-whacked face
32. her heightened color
33. her face was pale, but proud
34. face is deeply reddened
35. face white as chalk
36. wan face

37. dark face
38. white-faced
39. translucence of her face
40. sun-toughened face
41. his face was hard and very white

FA13 FACE 13 (OTHER)

1. his face was the upper-echelon Mafioso type
2. a familiar face
3. strain in her face
4. the stretch of facial muscles

HR
HAIR

HR1 HAIR 1

HR2 HAIR 2 (BALDING)

1. bald, except for a monkish fringe of white hair
2. sparse black hair
3. hair in middle-aged retreat
4. with ginger freckles on his bald skull
5. going bald in back
6. his slick locks combed sideways to conceal the tonsure

HR3 HAIR 3 (THICK)

1. full, dark hair, just graying at the temples
2. black hair in two thick shiny braids down to her waist
3. lustrous hair

4.   thick tresses which hung to her waist
5.   thatch of fair hair
6.   hair spread thickly over shoulders and down her back
7.   a shock of wheat-color hair
8.   a shock of woolly blond hair that need cutting
9.   his dark hair, just graying at the temples, was still full
10.   a thick black cap of wiry
11.   his full black hair flowed from his face like a crest
12.   thick sandy hair
13.   with a thick crop of yellow hair
14.   thick tawny-gold hair
15.   his thick hair tapering neatly to his collar
16.   she had a wealth of dark hair
17.   low hairline
18. her hair was a rich, glowing auburn
19.   the thickness of his hair
20.   thick and silky hair
21.   her hair was a rippling cloud
22.   tiny curling tendrils escaped the heavy silken mass of black hair
23.   a shock of hair
24.   thick head of hair
25.   a wealth of hair
26.   the heavy curtain of her hair

HR4 HAIR 4 (THIN)

1.   a mantle of long, thin white hair
2.   wispy white hair
3.   hair standing out in wisps around his head
4.   wispy bangs fell across her forehead
5.   her hair was a cobweb of silvery gold

HR5 HAIR 5 (LONG)

1.   the long blond-haired cheerleader type

2.   long golden tresses
3.   black hair in two thick shiny braids hung down to her waist
4.   thick tresses which hung to her waist
5.   long hair in loose braids
6.   hair spread thickly on her shoulders and down her back
7.   hair fell in a dark auburn curtain across
8.   hair falling in long plaits to her waist
9.   streaming silk of her hair
10.   hair falling uncurled down her back
11.   lank hair
12.   long braids
13.   length of her braids
14.   long auburn waves
15.   trailing hair
16.   tiny curling tendrils escaped the heavy silken mass of black hair
17.   great masses of curls
18.   dark hair fell in waves
19.   her hair tumbled carelessly down her back
20.   silver-blond hair worn straight and long
21.   her hair was a plume of black gold falling to her waist
22.   her long golden hair was like strands of lustrous glass
23.   hair fell to her waist
24.   a ragged mane of long blond hair
25.   a mantle of long, thin white hair
26.   her long disheveled hair dark against
27.   long, softly curling hair

HR 6 HAIR 6 (MEDIUM LENGTH)

1.   dark hair swinging about her proud shoulders
2.   cascaded over narrow shoulders like an unraveled floor mat
3.   her thick dark hair hung in long graceful curves over her shoulders
4.   great masses of curls

5. shoulder length hair
6. dark shoulder-length hair
7. great mane of hair
8. tiny curling tendrils escaped the heavy silken mass of black hair

HR7 HAIR 7 (SHORT)

1. her hair was a honey colored, curly cap
2. short-cropped hair
3. a thick black cap of wiry
4. red hair that spiked straight up
5. his dark curling hair was cut short
6. a big mound of sternly coifed beige hair
7. his full black hair flowed from his face like a crest
8. a razor haircut, stiff with spray
9. her hair, a tangerine pouf
10. a swath of wavy hair fell casually on his forehead
11. wispy bangs fell across her forehead
12. her hair was disheveled, a black aura encircling her head
13. tiny curling tendrils escaped the heavy silken mass of black hair
14. small curls twisted and crinkled across her forehead
15. wisps of hair framed her face
16. her ash-blonde hair clustered in short curls around a heart-shaped face
17. her head was capped by a mass of bronze-gold hair
18. copper ringlets curled on her forehead and on her nape
19. patch of hair
20. his thick hair tapering neatly to his collar
21. crew-cut
22. hair cut in the shape of an inverted bowl
23. hair stood straight up like wires

HR8 HAIR 8 (CURLY)

1.	bouncing hair
2.	irrepressible curly hair
3.	her head was capped by a mass of bronze-gold hair
4.	great masses of curls
5.	dark tendrils of hair curling on his forehead
6.	light brown curls were wind blown
7.	a fallen ringlet
8.	her hair tumbled carelessly down her back
9.	shiny brown hair with Medusa-style locks
10.	appallingly permed hair
11.	fine curly golden hair
12.	his dark curling hair was cut short
13.	her hair was a honey colored, curly cap
14.	frizzy-haired
15.	fine, curly, golden hair
16.	copper ringlets curled on her forehead and on her nape
17.	an escaping curl fell over her forehead
18.	small curls twisted and crinkled across her forehead
19.	a thick black cap of wiry hair
20.	her ash-blonde hair clustered in short curls around a heart-shaped face
21.	tumbled curls
22.	curly gray hair
23.	long, softly curling hair
24.	wiry red hair dusted with white

HR9 HAIR 9 (WAVY)

1.	her hair was a rippling cloud
2.	dark tendrils of hair curling on his forehead
3.	dark commas of hair
4.	a swath of wavy hair fell casually on his forehead
5.	her thick dark hair hung in long graceful curves over her shoulders

6.   his full black hair flowed from his face like a crest
7.   her hair tumbled carelessly down her back
8.   bouncing hair
9.   hair falling uncurled down her back
10.   long auburn waves
11.   stray tendrils of hair
12.   dark hair fell in waves
13.   intense unreal blackness of her iron-waved hair
14.   the immaculate wave of the woman's hair

HR10 HAIR 10 (STRAIGHT)

1.   her hair was a plume of black gold falling to her waist
2.   silver-blond hair worn straight and long
3.   a mantle of long, thin white hair
4.   her head was capped by a mass of bronze-gold hair
5.   his hair was black and silky straight
6.   lank hair

HR11 HAIR 11 (COARSE)

1.   rough black hair
2.   hair that had grown coarse with bleach
3.   a crisp mane of hair
4.   hair as stiff and black as a raven's wing
5.   crisp hair
6.   stiff hair
7.   frizzy-haired
8.   hair stood straight up like wires
9.   thatch of wild hair

HR12 HAIR 12 (FINE)

1.   his hair was the color of field oats

2.   a mantle of long, thin white hair
3.   hair as fine as gossamer
4.   fine curly golden hair
5.   his hair was black and silky straight
6.   wispy bangs fell across her forehead
7.   thick and silky hair
8.   streaming silk of her hair
9.   soft silk of her hair
10.   soft dark hair
11.   her hair was a cobweb of silvery gold
12.   downy hair

HR13 HAIR 13 (TANGLED)

1.   an unkempt head of hair
2.   disarrayed tangled hair
3.   hair was matted about her head and neck
4.   hair tangled about her face
5.   light brown curls were wind blown
6.   straggly hair
7.   silky tangles
8.   matted hair
9.   her hair was a cobweb of silvery gold
10.   her hair was disheveled, a black aura encircling her head
11.   his hair ruffled by the breeze
12.   her fair hair blown into disarray by the wind
13.   tangled mane of hair
14.   her long disheveled hair dark against

HR14 HAIR 14 (COLOR - BLONDE)

1.   delicate fair hair
2.   thick tawny-gold hair
3.   long golden tresses

4.   a golden head
5.   a shock of wheat-colored hair
6.   hair the color of warm honey
7.   mop of blond hair
8.   blissfully blond
9.   sun-washed blond hair
10.   fluffy blonde
11.   thick sandy hair
12.   the long blond-haired cheerleader type
13.   a big mound of sternly coifed beige hair
14.   fine curly golden hair
15.   a shock of woolly blond hair that need cutting
16.   her hair was the pale yellow of a field of grain
17.   the golden mist of her hair
18.   the silver swing of her hair
19.   silver-blond hair worn straight and long g
20.   with a thick crop of yellow hair
21.   his hair was the color of field oats
22.   fine, curly, golden hair
23.   her ash-blonde hair clustered in short curls around a heart-shaped face
24.   the white blond of an albino
25.   her hair was a luminous buttercup yellow
26.   his light hair was a stark contrast to his deep tan
27.   her hair was a honey colored, curly cap
28.   light, wheat-colored hair glistening with golden streaks
29.   a ragged mane of long blond hair
30.   her hair was a cobweb of silvery gold
31.   her long golden hair was like strands of lustrous glass
32.   a corona of glowing golden hair
33.   her head was capped by a mass of bronze-gold hair
34.   ginger-haired
35.   her fair hair blown into disarray by the wind
36.   dark gold hair
37.   flax-fair plaits
38.   his sandy hair was disarrayed and damp from the rain

HR15 HAIR 15 (COLOR - BROWN)

1. dark hair swinging about her proud shoulders
2. dark shoulder-length hair
3. his dark hair, just graying at the temples, was still full
4. dark commas of hair
5. thick sandy hair
6. shiny brown hair with Medusa-style locks
7. dark tendrils of hair curling on his forehead
8. his dark curling hair was cut short
9. his light brown hair had sandy-red highlights
10. her thick dark hair hung in long graceful curves over her shoulders
11. a wayward strand of dark hair
12. light brown curls were wind blown
13. luminous brown hair
14. her dark hair glistened like polished wood
15. she had a wealth of dark hair
16. dark gold hair
17. dark hair fell in waves
18. loose wisps of dark hair
19. soft dark hair
20. dark-haired
21. her long disheveled hair dark against

HR16 HAIR 16 (COLOR - BLACK)

1. dark tendrils of hair curling on his forehead
2. lustrous black hair
3. a thick veil of black hair
4. a thick black cap of wiry
5. her hair was a plume of black gold falling to her waist
6. black, unruly hair
7. hair as black as Manchester coal
8. hair as stiff and black as a raven's wing

9. his hair was black and silky straight
10. her hair was the black of a starless night
11. full, dark hair, just graying at the temples
12. her hair was disheveled, a black aura encircling her head
13. his dark hair, just graying at the temples, was still full
14. his full black hair flowed from his face like a crest
15. the jet-black hair flowed from a center part
16. his dark curling hair was cut short
17. his black hair gleamed in the lights
18. strong black hair
19. her dark hair glistened like polished wood
20. her hair was black, like shining glass
21. she had a wealth of dark hair
22. dark hair swinging about her proud shoulders
23. her thick dark hair hung in long graceful curves over her shoulders
24. loose wisps of dark hair
25. a wayward strand of dark hair
26. soft dark hair
27. rough black hair
28. dark shoulder-length hair
29. sleek black hair
30. dark-haired
31. dark commas of hair
32. dark hair fell in waves
33. her long disheveled hair dark against
34. intense unreal blackness of her iron-waved hair

HR17 HAIR 17 (COLOR - RED)

1. Red-gold hair
2. brass hair
3. firelight turned his hair into a glittering shower of flames
4. dark auburn hair spread thickly on her shoulders and down her back

5. her bright auburn hair gleamed with shadows of deep gold or rich red
6. dark red-gold hair that fell into her eyes
7. his hair ruddy bright
8. deep auburn hair shone bronze and gold from the sun
9. red hair that spiked straight up
10. her hair, a tangerine pouf
11. long auburn waves
12. hair the color of a fair sunset
13. his light brown hair had sandy-red highlights
14. her hair was a rich, glowing auburn
15. copper ringlets curled on her forehead and on her nape
16. wiry red hair dusted with white

HR18 HAIR 18 (COLOR - WHITE)

1. silvery hair
2. powder-white hair
3. the white blond of an albino
4. a mantle of long, thin white hair
5. her hair was a cobweb of silvery gold
6. wiry red hair dusted with white

HR19 HAIR 19 (COLOR - GRAY)

1. silvery hair
2. hair was stringy and gray
3. his hair was soot-gray and shaggy
4. dark hair, prematurely flecked with gray
5. long sideburns flecked with gray
6. his dark hair, just graying at the temples, was still full
7. full, dark hair, just graying at the temples
8. curly gray hair
9. prematurely flecked with gray

1. glimmer of her hair
2. long golden tresses
3. great hair
4. his hair was black and silky straight
5. her hair was a rich, glowing auburn
6. her dark hair glistened like polished wood
7. her hair was black, like shining glass
8. hair of good health
9. a wealth of hair
10. crisp hair
11. a ragged mane of long blond hair
12. sleek black hair
13. her hair was a luminous buttercup yellow
14. great mane of hair
15. tumbled curls
16. bouncing hair
17. soft dark hair
18. she had a wealth of dark hair
19. her long golden hair was like strands of lustrous glass
20. tiny curling tendrils escaped the heavy silken mass of black hair
21. her bright auburn hair gleamed with shadows of deep gold or rich red
22. her hair was a rippling cloud
23. her hair was a plume of black gold falling to her waist
24. dark hair swinging about her proud shoulders
25. strong black hair
26. streaming silk of her hair
27. a corona of glowing golden hair
28. a mantle of long, thin white hair
29. soft silk of her hair

HR21 HAIR 21 (UNHEALTHY)

1. oily hair
2. hair was stringy and gray
3. lank hair
4. appallingly permed hair
5. frizzy-haired
6. hair that had grown coarse with bleach
7. a ragged mane of long blond hair

HR22 HAIR 22 (STYLES)

1. a ragged mane of long blond hair
2. a mane of long, roughly cut tresses
3. long dark hair caught back with a silk scarf
4. hair brushed close to her head like a shining cap
5. hair was cut in a neat fringe across his eyes
6. hair tied back into an uncompromising ponytail that showed sharp angles of cheekbones
7. her hair fell loosely over her shoulders in an informal style
8. hair falling in long plaits to her waist
9. tumbled curls
10. her hair a perfect style for the richness of her clothes
11. a big mound of sternly coifed beige hair
12. his full black hair flowed from his face like a crest
13. each hair on his head lying obediently in place
14. wispy bangs fell across her forehead
15. carefully combed hair
16. long sideburns flecked with gray
17. neatly trimmed hair
18. unmanageable hair was another persistent problem of his life
19. a razor haircut, stiff with spray
20. hair cut in the shape of an inverted bowl
21. red hair that spiked straight up
22. his dark curling hair was cut short
23. tightly curled hair

24. long braids
25. unbound hair
26. appallingly permed hair
27. a cleaned0up hairdo
28. worn naturally
29. brush0shaped topknot
30. is thick hair tapering neatly to his collar
31. one lock fell a little forward onto his forehead
32. flax0fair plaits
33. length of her braids
34. the jet-black hair flowed from a center part
35. hair held back from his face by
36. wisps of hair framed her face
37. her head was capped by a mass of bronze-gold hair
38. looped braids
39. loosened hair
40. her hair was tied back severely with a black velvet ribbon
41. allowing her hair to fall loose over her shoulders

HR23 HAIR 23 (OTHER)

1. a loose thatch of hair across his forehead
2. a strong lock of hair
3. a strand of heavy dark hair
4. a wandering strand of hair
5. a flopping cowlick
6. a lock of hair
7. stray tendrils of hair
8. loose tendrils of hair softened her face
9. a wayward strand of dark hair
10. her hair loose across her face
11. his sandy hair was disarrayed and damp from riding in the rain

BE
BEARDS

BE1 BEARDS 1

1. Grey-beard
2. a day's growth of beard
3. unshaven stubble
4. fringed beard
5. the shadow of his beard
6. brown-bearded
7. long and knotted beard
8. bushy whiskers
9. beard of wiry hair
10. tightly curled beard
11. beard clipped to a point
12. curled beard
13. Sikh style rolled beard
14. whiskbroom beard

MS
MOUSTACHE
MS1 MOUSTACHE 1

1. a wispy mustache that would never be anything but wispy
2. heavily mustached lips
3. a thin, carefully clipped mustache
4. a long, drooping mustache
5. a white walrus mustache
6. an umbrella of a mustache

SK
SKIN

SK1 SKIN 1 (COLOR - TAN)

1. Sun-whacked skin

2.   evenly tanned save for the slight bikini mark
3.   sun-seared skin
4.   sun-bronzed skin
5.   deeply tanned

SK2 SKIN 2 (COLOR - AVERAGE)

1.   smooth olive skin
2.   her skin was like peach-tinted cream
3.   a golden tan
4.   honey-colored skin
5.   the apricot and milky color of her skin

SK3 SKIN 3 (COLOR - LIGHT)

1.   had gone very white
2.   angelic coloring
3.   a beautiful china-skinned blond girl
4.   a grayish pallor under his skin
5.   milk-fed skin
6.   her skin was like peach-tinted cream
7.   he had the pallor of desk work
8.   her soft ivory skin
9.   porcelain-pale
10. a camellia-like complexion
11. creamy skin
12. soft ivory flesh
13. her color was poor
14. fair-skinned
15. too fair-skinned
16. Warm clear skin
17. the apricot and milky color of her skin

SK4 SKIN 4 (COLOR - WHITE)

1.   Fish-belly white

SK5 SKIN 5 (COLOR - FRECKLES)

1.   freckles on her
2.   a dusting of freckles on her cheeks

SK6 SKIN 6 (COLOR - PINK)

1.   a new, pinkish skin, like that of a baby

SK7 SKIN 7 (COLOR - BLACK)

1.   skin as dark and shiny as black chintz

SK8 SKIN 8 (COLOR - YELLOW)

1.   a golden tan
2.   a high-yellow Negro
3.   smooth olive skin
4.   honey-colored skin
5.   skin was sickly pallid under its weathering
6.   a bit sallow

SK9 SKIN 9 (COLOR - RED)

1.   Sun-whacked skin
2.   a dusky red flush
3.   sun-seared skin
4.   red-brown skin
5.   an angry burn

6.   ruddy complexion
7.   Warm clear skin

SK10 SKIN 10 (COLOR - BROWN)

1.   Sun-whacked skin
2.   sun-seared skin
3.   a golden tan
4.   red-bronze tan
5.   his light hair was a stark contrast to his deep tan
6.   a sizzling girl of summer
7.   sun glowing
8.   red-brown skin
9.   deeply tanned

SK11 SKIN 11 (TEXTURE - WRINKLED)

1.   a network of tiny lines
2.   two deep lines of worry
3.   lines of concentration
4.   skin was so wrinkled it almost buried her features
5.   a web of wrinkles
6.   he was gray-white and toughened like a dry hide
7.   featherlike laugh lines
8.   sun-toughened skin
9.   a complex set of wrinkles
10.   a gorgeous battlefield of wrinkles
11.   as shriveled as an old orange
12.   sun-whacked skin

SK12 SKIN 12 (TEXTURE - ROUGH)

1.   his troubled face was like a graveled parking lot
2.   skin was sickly pallid under its weathering
3.   sun-whacked skin

4.   he was gray-white and toughened like a dry hide
5.   his rough skin
6.   sun-toughened skin

SK13 SKIN 13 (TEXTURE - SMOOTH)

1.   the flesh of his body had the warm sleekness of silk
2.   clean shaven
3.   smooth olive skin
4.   sleek with fat
5.   her skin smooth and sweet-smelling
6.   with all the bloom of youth
7.   creamy skin
8.   so fresh and excited that she gleamed
9.   warm clear skin

SK14 SKIN 14 (TEXTURE - SOFT)

1.   the flesh of his body had the warm sleekness of silk
2.   soft flesh
3.   soft ivory flesh

SK15 SKIN 15 (HEALTHY)

1.   she was clean, tidy and unapproachable
2.   healthy glow of life

SK16 SKIN 16 (UNHEALTHY)

1.   color had drained from her face making her hair darker than
       ever
2.   straight brows were black ink against the pallor of her skin
3.   skin pallor was more noticeable by the blush of her lips

SK17 SKIN 17 (LOCATION)

1. over her skin
2. bare skin of her back
3. bare skin of her shoulders

SK18 SKIN 18 (HOT)

1. an angry burn
2. awash with sweat
3. skin grew hot as if he were basting naked on a spit
4. forehead was damp and ice cold and hands were burning hot
5. the heat of his touch
6. warm flesh

SK19 SKIN 19 (WARM)

1. soft warmth of her body

SK20 SKIN 20 (COLD)

1. a shiver of cold down her spine

SK21 SKIN 21 (PERSPIRATION)

1. sweaty sheen
2. awash with sweat
3. pouring with sweat
4. beads of perspiration standing out on
5. soaked to the skin with exertion
6. perspiration on her forehead, like water beads on good butter
7. a film of sweat on her face
8. beads of sweat

9. sweat-shiny

SK22 SKIN 22 (SENSATIONS)

1. tingling skin
2. flushing slightly with pleasure

SK23 SKIN 23 (OTHER)

1. ginger freckles

FH
FOREHEAD

FH1 FOREHEAD 1

1. smooth brow
2. her brow was high and rounded
3. across her forehead
4. deep furrowed lines across the forehead
5. a square wall of a forehead with heavy brows for a base
6. his brow was dark
7. forehead beaded with sweat
8. a sharp furrow
9. high forehead
10. broad forehead
11. faint lines on a smooth brow
12. noble brow
13. a tiny frown-crease in her smooth forehead
14. furrows in his forehead
15. back from his brow
16. off his forehead
17. on his forehead
18. across his forehead
19. furrowed brow

FH2 FOREHEAD 2 (TEMPLE)

1.   on her temple

EY
EYES

EY1 EYES 1

EY2 EYES 2 (AGE - YOUNG)

1.   guiless stare
2.   the eyes of a carefree girl
3.   new eyes
4.   ingenious eyes

EY3 EYES 3 (AGE - OLD)

1.   eyes ten thousand years old
2.   eyes were sunk in the pallid hollow of his face
3.   tired old eyes

EY4 EYES 4 (AESTHETICS - BEAUTY)

1.   looked scholarly in glasses
2.   extraordinary eyes
3.   sweet eyes
4.   the eyes were compelling, magnetic
5.   her most remarkable feature.
6.   luminous, slightly protuberant green eyes
7.   his eyes were different
8.   lovely eyes

9.   liquid eyes
10. dreamy eyes
11. eyes were twins of incredible beauty
12. eyes had luster
   13. eyes of a poet

EY5 EYES 5 (AESTHETICS - UGLY)

1.   his eyes were different
2.   drooping eye
3.   eerie, piercing eyes
4.   rheumy-eyed
5.   hard, gelatin eyes
6.   tired old eyes
7.   boggling eyes

EY6 EYES 6 (HEALTHY)

1.   his sharp eyes
2.   keen-sighted eye
3.   eyes had luster
4.   keenly observant eye
5.   eagle-eye
6.   keen eyes
7.   sharp-eyed

EY7 EYES 7 (UNHEALTHY)

1.   dark smudges beneath her eyes
2.   eyes were dry and somewhat feverish
3.   exhausted eyes
4.   vacant pink-rimmed eyes
5.   shadows beneath her eyes
6.   eyes were shadowed from the lack of sleep
7.   eyes were heavy from lack of sleep

8. dark rings beneath his eyes
9. her eyes shadowed and huge
10. there was a veil of blood before her eyes
11. bleary-eyed
12. puffed eyes
13. swimming eyes
14. eye was hard-pressed
15. strained gaze
16. death-bright eyes
17. feral eyes
18. eyes blurred with sleep
19. sick eyes
20. glazed eyes
21. death-bright eyes
22. rheumy-eyed
23. her huge eyes accentuated by the shadows beneath them
24. dark rings under her eyes

EY8 EYES 8 (EXPRESSIONS - NEGATIVE)

1. angry eyes
2. nervous sidelong glances
3. a smoldering look
4. a hot glance
5. a keep-your-mouth-shut look
6. a withering glance angry gaze
7. a murderous glance
8. a devilish look
9. mischievous look
10. a strange, faintly eager look
11. tortured eyes maddening leer
12. wild-eyed
13. steely glare
14. interrogatory gaze
15. a suggestive look

16. a speculative glance
17. eyes flashing sparks
18. suspicious eyes
19. a gaze of cruelty
20. guarded look in her eyes
21. a withering look
22. eyes were stony with suspicion
23. a piercing glance
24. eyes were very shrewd
25. uncompromising gaze
26. the pupils were very small her eyes weary but resolute
27. taunting eyes
28. sad eyes
29. his eyes were dark and insolent
30. eyes instinctively on guard, like a pit bull in a ring
31. impatient brown eyes
32. inimical (hostile) gaze
33. wistful eyes
34. bolting eyes
35. terrifying eyes
36. her wide-eyed innocence was merely a smoke screen
37. his eyes were cold and proud
38. granite eyes
39. grave eyes
40. his stare was bold
41. a look of disdain
42. a look that made the breath leave her body
43. her eyes were full of remoteness
44. trained eyes
45. chilling gaze
46. restless eyes
47. intent stare
48. the set glare of his eyes
49. his eyes were fixed
50. cool eyes
51. a flicker of annoyance

52. hardened eyes
53. a flicker of surprise
54. perplexed look
55. boggling eyes
56. flinty eyes
57. the eyes were hostile
58. a single sharp look
59. restless eyes
60. eyes on guard
61. under the malevolent gaze
62. a look of worship
63. intimidating glare
64. an expression of awe
65. a piercing glance
66. probing eyes
67. challenging look
68. dangerous looks
69. voracious eyes
70. mooningly worshipful eyes
71. watchful-wary eyes
72. strangest haunted look
73. disturbing eyes
74. intense stare
75. arch glance
76. sly leer
77. mooning expressions
78. grave eyes
79. questioning gaze
80. a black look
81. mooning expressions
82. eyes slits of blazing rage
83. inescapably appraising eyes
84. troubled eyes
85. a contemptuous flickering glance
86. frosty eyes
87. her expression intense

88. a lingering look
89. a sly look
90. a look of suspicion
91. eyes were as watchful as those of a man facing a death peril
92.   eyes were guarded
93.   the set glare of his eyes
94.   eyes of a man used to giving orders
95.   bleak eyes
96.   wintry glare
97.   a narrow look
98.   that knowing look
99.   withering stare
100.   her eyes were a blue-eyed vise
101.   eyes that blurred with perpetual indecision
102.   with a tinge of sadness in her eyes
103.   large, timid eyes
104.   eyes like talons
105.   brutal and unfriendly stare
106.   compelling eyes
107.   a penetrating look
108.   double meaning of his gaze
109.   his eyes were different
110.   burning reproachful eyes
111.   a cold look
112.   a hostile glare
113.   a calculating expression
114.   a narrowed glinting glance
115.   a cool appraising look
116.   icy gaze
117.   mystery in his eyes
118.   rapier glance
119.   critical squint
120.   a pair of icy blue eyes radiated hatred and torment
121.   dark eyes with a sort of reserve he couldn't place
122.   there was something lazily seductive in his look
123.   raking gaze

---

124. a black layered look
125. eyes, which by the dint of pure stupid instinct, were fearless
126. a commanding look
127. eyes large and fierce with pain
128. eyes alight like a fire, somewhat like an arsonist's
129. there was a lethal calmness in his eyes
130. her eyes were stony with anger
131. his eyes were filled with contempt
132. his eyes were hard and filled with dislike
133. his eyes were full of half promises
134. twitching mechanical eyes
135. bold black eyes. . .defiant
136. a wounded look in her dark eyes
137. his eyes were hard and cruel and pitiless
138. speculative gaze
139. her eyes clouded with hazy sadness
140. hard, gelatin eyes
141. a quick, denying glance
142. her eyes were pools of appeal
143. gaze is carefully candid
144. his eyes strangely veiled
145. a worried eye

EY9 EYES 9 (EXPRESSIONS - NONE)

1. eyes curiously dead
2. eyes were uncomprehending
3. eyes like a sleepwalkers
4. vacant pink-rimmed
5. the narrowest range of inflection
6. faraway look
7. gaze was focused on the middle distance
8. blank eyes which gave nothing away
9. her eyes clouded with visions of the past
10. his eyes were bemused and opaque

11. blankness of his eyes
12. his eyes were flat, hard, passionless
13. with a blank animal eye
14. blank bewilderment in his eyes
15. eyes were as indecipherable as water
16. his eyes were icy and unresponsive
17. blank-television stare
18. blank-eyed
19. flat, unspeaking eyes
20. strangest unreadable expression
21. a deadpan stare
22. his eyes were dark and unfathomable
23. toneless stare
24. the olive-black eyes, unfathomable in their murky depths
25. unexpressive eyes
26. utterly vacant eyes
27. watery eyes with absolutely no expression
28. vacant orbs
29. eyes were blank
30. dullness of her eyes

EY10 EYES 10 (EXPRESSIONS - POSITIVE)

1. wistful eyes
2. a look of satisfied contentment
3. a devilish look
4. a mischievous look
5. a look of intense, clear light in her eyes
6. smile in his eyes
7. glowed with luminous intelligence
8. twinkled with humor
9. crackled with emotion
10. gaze held both merriment and exasperation
11. intelligence in her gaze
12. assessing look in her eyes

13. eyes gleamed with excitement
14. a old fashioned look
15. laughing hazel eyes
16. eyes were round with importance
   17. her large blue eyes vivid and questioning
   18. there was something lazily seductive in his look
   19. he had clear, observant eyes
   20. eager look
   21. his eyes were brilliantly intelligent
   22. his warm gold-green eyes were full of expectation
   23. her eyes were artless and serene
   24. her eyes were filled with a curious deep longing
   25. his eyes brimmed with tenderness and passion
   26. the eyes were gentle and contemplative
   27. there was eagerness in his eyes
   28. a subtle look of amusement
   29. his eyes had a sheen of purpose
   30. mystery in his eyes
   31. wise little eyes, bright and bemused
   32. his eyes glowed with a savage inner fire
   33. there was a faint glint of hurt in his eyes
   34. his eyes were bright with merriment
   35. his eyes were sharp and assessing
   36. his eyes showed intelligence and independence of spirit
   37. her blue eyes were full of life, pain, and unquenchable warmth
   38. inquisitive raisin-brown eyes
   39. enigmatic gaze
   40. ingenious eyes
   41. gaze as soft as a caress
   42. straight glance
   43. his appreciative eye
   44. an approving glance
   45. his stare was bold
   46. keenly observant eye
   47. speculative gaze

48. sweet musing look
49. practiced masculine eye
50. a frank and admiring look
51. a look that made the breath leave her body
52. new eyes
53. trained eyes
54. steady gaze
55. earnest eyes
56. a commanding look
57. a penetrating look
58. her eyes were the beautiful blue of a robin's eggs and had just as much expression
59. dreamy eyes
60. heartrending tenderness of his gaze
61. lively eyes
62. that knowing look
63. curious looks
64. a questioning look
65. her eyes were pools of appeal
66. look which contained intelligence
67. a look of worship
68. grave eyes
69. guiless stare
70. a worried eye
71. his look was galvanizing
72. compelling eyes
73. a lingering look
74. soft, dark watchful eyes that missed nothing
75. a flicker of surprise
76. eyes were steady
77. probing eyes
78. peaceful eyes
79. light of reason in his eyes
80. a flash of concern
81. intent stare
82. a look of amusement

83. eyes as clever as a terrier's
84. eyes which held one on the balance scale
85. challenging look
86. contented eyes
87. a confiding look
88. excitement in his eye
89. his deep eyes showed the sensitivity of a scholar
90. kindly eyes
91. questioning gaze
92. her look confident
93. inescapably appraising eyes
94. a long, wide-eyed stare
95. intense stare
96. a lazy laughter in his eyes
97. inquisitive glance
98. an odd mingling wariness and amusement in his eyes
99. one smiling glance
100. his eyes were different
101. her expression intense
102. astonished eyes
103. piercing yet merry eyes
104. there was always laughter in his eyes
105. curious look

EY11 EYES 11 (OTHER)

1. clear sight
2. all-seeing eyes
3. eyes seemed to be the only thing alive about her
4. the look of a milk-fed calf
5. eyes that could kindle wet leaves
6. seeking eyes
7. a fleeting glance
8. the sensitive, inspired eye of the artist
9. a concentrated stare

10.   Indian eyes
11.   eyes ahead

EY12 EYES 12 (SHAPES - LARGE)

1.   wide-eyed astonishment
2.   she had full hazel eyes with sweeping lashes
3.   her large blue eyes vivid and questioning
4.   large black eyes
5.   eyes were wide
6.   large, timid eyes
7.   moon-eyed
8.   big, droopy eyes
9.   wide-eyed
10. eyes were enormous
11. the eyes of a doe

EY13 EYES 13 (SHAPES - SMALL)

1.   little turtle brown eyes
2.   little eyes
3.   his eyes were little blue chinks in a set face
4.   wise little eyes, bright and bemused
5.   eyes were shrewd little chips of quartz
6.   piggy eyes
7.   beady eyes

EY14 EYES 14 (SHAPES - ROUND)

1.   Wide-eyed astonishment
2.   little turtle brown eyes
3.   snakelike eyes
4.   round eyes

5. owlish eyes
6. eyes like balls of shattered blue marble
7. moon-eyed
8. goggling eyes
9. beady eyes
10. piggy eyes
11. goggle-eyed
12. with rounded eyes

EY15 EYES 15 (SHAPES - NARROW)

1. Smoky-blue eyes that tilted catlike
2. Narrow-eyed alertness
3. eyes were slits
4. crinkling eyes
5. eyes were almond and slanted
6. narrowed eyes
7. slitted eyes of a mountain lion

EY16 EYES 16 (SHAPES – DEEP SET)

1. his deep eyes showed the sensitivity of a scholar
2. so deep-set and intense that he could not be sure of their color
3. eyes set off in deep shadowed sockets
4. deep-set eyes

EY17 EYES 17 (SHAPES - BULGING)

1. goggling eyes
2. prominent green eyes
3. protruding eyes shadowed by thick brows
4. slightly protruding coffee-brown eyes
5. slightly protuberant eyes
6. goggle-eyed

EY18 EYES 18 (SHAPES - OTHER)

1. eyes resembled pale stones on a wintry beach
2. eyes were shrewd little chips of quartz
3. eyes like a terrier
4. boar-hog eyes
5. eyes of a feline
6. hawk-like eyes
7. owlish eyes
8. little turtle brown eyes
9. smoky-blue eyes that tilted catlike
10. eyes like a wolf
11. slitted pupils

EY19 EYES 19 (LOCATION)

1. sidelong glance
2. between his lashes
3. far back in her eyes
4. the corners of his eyes
5. in the shadow of her eyes
6. within her eyes
7. line of sight
8. a tilted eyeball socket
9. toward the corner of the eye
10. just behind the eyeballs
11. behind her eyes
12. out of the corner of his eye
13. blue eyes hidden under thick, yellow brows
14. a sideways look
15. there were liquid blue shadows in her eyes
16. a half-glance
17. backward glance

18. straight in the eye
19. back in those eyes
20. in the smoldering depths of his eyes
21. his visual sphere
22. in their sockets
23. pockets under her eyes
24. along the outer edge of the eye
25. with the tail of his eye
26. eyes ahead
27. through hindsight's eye
28. eyes ahead
29. hindsight's vision
30. a sidelong view
31. eyes set far apart
32. a sidelong glance
33. dark rings under her eyes

EY20 EYES 20 (LOCATION - UNDER THE EYES)

1. a shadow of fatigue under the eyes
2. shadows beneath her eyes
3. dark baggy wrinkles under his eyes
4. deeply shadowed around the eyes
5. eyes were ringed with dark circles
6. pockets under her eyes

EY21 EYES 21 (EYELIDS)

1. an oddly reptilian blink
2. a wet eyelid
3. eyelids felt like iron shutters
4. against the backs of her eyelids
5. blinked like a dyspeptic halibut
6. closed wet eyes

7. red-rimmed from the cold
8. beneath her lids
9. big, droopy eyes
10. half-closed jade green eyes
11. vampy, heavy-lidded eyes
12. sloe-eyed, half-asleep
13. his eyes were hooded like those of a hawk
14. eyes hooded
15. down-dropped lids
16. downcast eyes
17. lowered lids
18. veiled, liquid eyes
19. eyes were ringed with dark circles
20. veiled eyes
21. sleepy-eyed
22. eyes fast shut
23. eyes shut tight
24. long-lidded eyes
25. tinted lids
26. eyes low and demure
27. tight shut lids
28. wet eyelid
29. deep shadow of his eyes
30. brilliant eyes that would not shut
31. maiden-like demureness
32. half-closed lids
33. smirking wink
34. exaggerated wink
35. his tiny fringed eyelids

EY22 EYES 22 (COLOR - BLUE)

1. eyes a blue blaze of memory
2. a blue flame of defiance in her eyes
3. there was a pale blue between his lashes
4. mellow blue eyes

5. dark blue
6. eyes of gentian blue
7. china blue
8. deep blue-black eyes
9. blue eyes with thick, sooty lashes
10. her blue eyes shone like cobalt
11. his wild sapphire eyes
12. his eyes were a brilliant blue
13. clean blue eyes were deeply set under prominent brows
14. the Nordic blue of his eyes
15. hazel eyes with golden rims
16. her blue eyes were full of life, pain, and unquenchable warmth
17. wild, exotic sapphire eyes
18. his eyes were little blue chinks in a set face
19. eyes like balls of shattered blue marble
20. faded dust blue eyes
21. a pair of icy blue eyes radiated hatred and torment
22. dark eyebrows arching over winter-blue eyes
23. sea-blue eyes
24. her eyes were the beautiful blue of a robin's eggs and had just as much expression
25. blue eyes hidden under thick, yellow brows
26. blue flecked with gray
27. she had clear blue eyes ringed with black lashes
28. compelling blue eyes
29. there were liquid blue shadows in her eyes
30. eyes that were a startling blue, as blue as the summer sky
31. great blue eyes
32. the blue of his eyes was like a cold wave
33. her bright, clear blue eyes were direct
34. her blue eyes flashed with azure fire
35. her eyes were pale blue with a splash of green
36. the sunlight in his blue eyes shone like bits of gleaming porcelain
37. her large blue eyes vivid and questioning
38. smoky-blue eyes that tilted catlike

39.   the rare beauty of violet eyes
40.   ocean-blue eyes
41.   blue eyes fired with topaz
42.   startlingly blue eyes
43.   his eyes were even darker than sapphires

EY23 EYES 23 (COLOR - BROWN)

1.   limpid brown eyes
2.   amber fire in his eyes
3.   soft brown eyes golden eyes
4.   eyes were brown as hazelnuts and very shrewd
5.   his eyes were shades of amber and green
6.   his eyes were an entrancing chocolate brown
7.   liquid brown eyes
8.   her hazel eyes were lit from within with a golden glow
9.   intense brown eyes
10.   her eyes like a stream of gold in the dark
11.   inquisitive raisin-brown eyes
12.   hazel eyes with golden rims
13.   slightly protruding coffee-brown eyes
14.   cold brown eyes
15.   fox-colored eyes
16.   his eyes were a tawny shade of brown
17.   little turtle brown eyes
18.   dark brown eyes

EY24 EYES 24 (COLOR - VIOLET)

1.   the eyes swept with violet
2.   the rare beauty of violet eyes

EY25 EYES 25 (COLOR - GREEN)

1. Green-gilt eyes
2. country green eyes
3. clear, light green eyes strange green eyes
4. flecked with gold
5. laughing hazel eyes   cool green eyes with strange amber flecks
6. her most remarkable feature. . .luminous, slightly protuberant green eyes
7. warm gold-green eyes
8. dark gray-green flecked eyes
9. his eyes were shades of amber and green
10. her hazel eyes were lit from within with a golden glow
11. she had large green eyes under golden brows and lashes
12. the olive-black eyes, unfathomable in their murky depths
13. green-gold eyes
14. her eyes were like green, polished jade
15. he had eyes like green ice
16. the shifting emerald lights of her eyes
17. clear green eyes
18. bottle green eyes
19. jade-spoked eyes
20. eyes were like chipped emeralds
21. jade green eyes
22. hazel eyes with golden rims
23. eyes were a quick gray green
24. her eyes were pale blue with a splash of green

EY26 EYES 26 (COLOR - BLACK)

1. her dark eyes were as beautiful as black satin
2. luminous jet-black eyes
3. deep-set jet black eyes
4. brilliant black button eyes
5. the olive-black eyes, unfathomable in their murky depths
6. eyes like clear black glass
7. the eyes like black holes in the pale face

8.   inky blackness of his eyes
9.   bold black eyes
10. anthracite eyes
11. he had depthless, jet-black eyes
12. currant-black eyes
13. large black eyes
14. eyes like coals
15. his eyes were obsidian black

EY27 EYES 27 (COLOR - RED)

1.   eyes like harsh sparks in the light
2.   eyes were red and puffy
3.   eyes like coals
4.   red-rimmed eyes
5.   bloodshot eyes
6.   eyes blazing red

EY28 EYES 28 (COLOR - DARK)

1.   eyes like coals
2.   his eyes were as dark and powerful as he was
3.   her dark eyes reflected glimmers of light
4.   dark snappy eyes
5.   her dark eyes were as beautiful as black satin
6.   eyes were ringed with dark circles
7.   dark eyes framing a handsome square face
8.   his dark eyes were hazy
9.   dark gray-green flecked eyes
10. eyes so dark that the iris and pupil blended
11. his eyes were even darker than sapphires
12. soft, dark watchful eyes that missed nothing
13. dark burning eyes
14. inky blackness of his eyes
15. dark-eyed

EY29 EYES 29 (COLOR - BRIGHT)

1. the sunlight in his blue eyes shone like bits of gleaming porcelain
2. amber fire in his eyes
3. piercingly bright dark eyes
4. her hazel eyes were lit from within with a golden glow
5. his eyes gleamed like glassy volcanic rock
6. his eyes had a sheen of purpose
7. her eyes held a gleam that no makeup could improve
8. her green eyes lighted a little
9. dark burning eyes
10. brilliant black button eyes
11. the shifting emerald lights of her eyes
12. eyes like coals
13. her blue eyes flashed with azure fire
14. eyes alight like a fire, somewhat like an arsonist's
15. her eyes had a burning, faraway look in them
16. his eyes were like summer lightning
17. his eyes were brilliantly intelligent
18. with a glint of wonder in his eyes
19. unspoken pain was alive and glowing in his eyes
20. an almost hopeful glint in his eyes
21. there was a spark of some indefinable emotion in his eyes
22. the excited light was vivid in her eyes
23. a twinkle of moonlight caught his eyes
24. a gleam of interest in his gray eyes
25. his eyes were bight with merriment
26. his eyes glowed with a savage inner fire
27. death-bright eyes
28. too bright eyes
29. her most remarkable feature. . .luminous, slightly protuberant green eyes
30. amber flames in his eyes
31. eyes uncannily aglow

32. eyes like clear black glass
33. a twinkling look
34. her eyes were mirror brilliant
35. very bright eyes
36. eyes like harsh sparks in the light
37. a gleaming in his eye
38. dark snappy eyes
39. gleaming eyed
40. the brilliance of his look
41. his burning eyes
42. preternaturally bright eyes
43. glitter of his eyes
44. a bright glance
45. a gleam of appreciation
46. her eyes shimmered with the light from the window
47. her dark eyes reflected glimmers of light
48. a canny glint
49. his gray eyes were like silver lightning
50. clear glow of his eyes
51. eyes had luster
52. glint in his eye

EY30 EYES 30 (COLOR - WHITE)
1. whites of her eyes
2. the whites of the man's eyes
3. white-rimmed with terror

EY31 EYES 31 (COLOR - GRAY)

1. disconcertingly intense gray eyes
2. gray eyes like the thunderclouds
3. quick gray eyes
4. blue flecked with gray
5. his gray eyes were like silver lightning

6.   eyes the color of gun metal
7.   granite eyes
8.   hard, gray eyes, like glacial ice
9.   eyes were a quick gray green
10.   dark gray-green flecked eyes
11.   huge eyes light gray, with radiating streaks in the irises

EY32 EYES 32 (COLOR - DULL)

1.   his eyes were covered with a milky translucent film
2.   his eyes were bemused and opaque
3.   flat, unspeaking eyes
4.   his eyes were flat, hard, passionless

EY33 EYES 33 (COLOR - OTHER)

1.   he had extraordinary eyes, flecked and ringed with gold
2.   golden eyes
3.   the gold in his eyes flickered with interest
4.   gold-flecked eyes

EY34 EYES 34 (WITH EYEGLASSES)

1.   his eyes encased in thick spectacles
2.   looked scholarly in glasses
3.   behind the thick lenses
4.   her eyes, intense behind the large square lenses of her glasses
5.   eyes magnified a little by the thick lenses of his glasses
6.   his glasses in his hand
7.   a ridge at the bridge of his nose where his glasses had trenched

EY35 EYES 35 (TEARS)

1. her eyes were misty and wistful
2. hot tear
3. tears of pleasure
4. hot exultant tear
5. tears of frustration
6. two lone tears appeared beneath her lashes
7. closed wet eyes
8. huge tears
9. eyes were red and puffy
10. her eyes bright with tears
11. eyes were full of tears
12. a thin rope of tears
13. her eyes clouded with hazy sadness
14. watery eyes with absolutely no expression
15. red-rimmed eyes
16. puffed eyes
17. veiled, liquid eyes
18. eyes were misty
19. dark fearful tears
20. signs of tears
21. a burst of tears
22. a small brush with tears
23. huge teardrops
24. ready tears

EY36 EYES 36 (EYEBROWS)

1. clean blue eyes were deeply set under prominent brows
2. sliver-thin eyebrows
3. arched eyebrows
4. well-marked brows
5. fine, arched eyebrows
6. fine, silky eyebrows
7. triangular brows

8. knitted eyebrows
9. craggy brows
10. along his brow dark eyebrows
11. drawn brows
12. an ironic eyebrow
13. straight brows were black ink against the pallor of her skin
14. slim arched brows
15. a slant to the brows
16. blue eyes hidden under thick, yellow brows
17. slight lift of the brows
18. a square wall of a forehead with heavy brows for a base
19. protruding eyes shadowed by thick brows
20. she had large green eyes under golden brows and lashes
21. iron-brown eyebrows
22. dark eyebrows arching over winter-blue eyes
23. shaggy brows
24. bushy eyebrows
25. straight brows
26. thin brows
27. a lofty cocky eyebrow
28. well-marked black brows
29. narrowly plucked eyebrows

EY37 EYES 37 (EYELASHES)

1. she had full hazel eyes with sweeping lashes
2. there was a pale blue between his lashes
3. through her eyelashes
4. two lone tears appeared beneath her lashes
5. short sandy lashes
6. tiny fringed lids
7. thick, sooty lashes
8. Cute eyelashes
9. Long-lashed eyes
10. she had clear blue eyes ringed with black lashes

11.   heavy lashes
12. she had large green eyes under golden brows and lashes
13. thick, black lashes
14. fringe of her lashes
15. lowered lashes
16. his tiny fringed eyelids
17. under her eyelashes
18. fringed with dark-red lashes

ER
EARS

ER1 EARS 1

1. the public ear
2. her earlobe
3. out of the corner of her ears   against her ear
4. to his ears
5. from her ears
6. tiny ears as delicate as rose petals
7. his ear to her chest
8. could hear her own heartbeats drumming in her ears
9. beneath her ears
10. perky ears
11. rose petal ears
12. out of earshot
13. big ears
14. the mind's ear
15. behind each ear
16. the corner of her ears
17. outsized ears

NO
NOSE

NO1 NOSE 1

NO2 NOSE 2 (LARGE)

1. a nose the size and color of an apple
2. bulbous nose
3. huge warty nose
4. prominent patrician nose
5. heavy nose

NO3 NOSE 3 (SMALL)

1. little jutting nose
2. button nose
3. pert nose
4. her nose was exquisitely dainty

NO4 NOSE 4 (WIDE)

1. heavy nose
2. broad nose
3. his nose looked like a wedge of cheddar
4. widened nostrils

NO5 NOSE 5 (NARROW)

1. her nose was exquisitely dainty
2. long thin missionary's nose
3. finely cut nostrils
4. pointed nose
5. fine nose
6. her nose was slender and fine and the nostrils delicate
7. his nose was long and fine
8. delicate nostrils
9. slender nose

10.   aquiline nose
11.   thin nose

NO6 NOSE 6 (LONG)

1.   boldly arched nose
2.   a slight bend in a nose unusually long
3.   long nose

NO7 NOSE 7 (SHORT)

1.   nose was a little too short
2.   pert nose
3.   a snub nose
4.   her nose was straight, short and charming
5.   sort of snub-nosed
6.   little jutting nose
7.   pug nose

NO8 NOSE 8 (LOCATION)

1.   along the vector of his nose
2.   nostrils
3.   tip of her nose
4.   from his nostrils
5.   in front of her nose
6.   against his nose
7.   beneath her nose
8.   a ridge at the bridge of his nose where his glasses had trenched
9.   down the wings of her nose
10.   taut lines between her nose and mouth

NO9 NOSE 9 (OTHER)

1. peeling nose
2. crooked nose
3. nose curved like scimitar
4. slightly arched nose
5. bent nose
6. a blowing of her nose
7. her pretty Grecian nose
8. nose was reddened

NO10 NOSE 10 (NOSTRILS)

1. finely cut nostrils
2. flare of her nostrils
3. hairy nostril
4. elliptic nostrils
5. keen nostrils

CH
CHEEKS

CH1 CHEEKS 1

CH2 CHEEKS 2 (LOCATION)

1. a trace of rouge on her cheeks
2. against his cheek
3. down his cheeks
4. cheek muscles
5. elegant ridge of his cheekbones
6. from his cheek to his jaw-line
7. the line of her cheekbone and jaw two dimples on her cheeks
8. along the side of her cheek
9. down her cheeks
10. high cheekbones

11.   high planes of her cheekbones
12. pronounced cheekbones
13. cheeks displayed unhealthy little roses as the blood drained out of them
14. elegant ridge of his cheekbones
15. she had a musk-rose flush on her ivory cheekbones
16. an unwelcome blush on her cheeks
17. a blush of pleasure on her cheeks
18. dusky color on her cheeks
19. a blush like a shadow on her cheeks
20. stains of scarlet on his cheeks
21. across her cheekbones

CH3 CHEEKS 3 (COLOR)

1. Pink-stained cheeks
2. reddened cheeks
3. her soft cheeks were rose and pearl
4. rosy-cheeked
5. the flush on her pale cheek was like the flush of sunset on snow
6. dusky color on her cheeks
7. white cheeks
8. stains of scarlet on his cheeks
9. a blush like a shadow on her cheeks
10. she had a musk-rose flush on her ivory cheekbones
11. the dusty rose of her cheeks
12. cheeks displayed unhealthy little roses as the blood drained out of them
13. an unwelcome blush on her cheeks
14. a blush of pleasure on her cheeks
15. cheeks were vivid scarlet
16. a trace of rouge on her cheeks
17. aflame with blushes
18. crimson cheeks
19. flushed cheeks
20. unwonted flush of her cheeks

21. glowing cheeks
22. apple-cheeked
23. cheeks were flame-hot

CH4 CHEEKS 4 (OTHER)

1. taut, bony cheeks
2. burning cheeks
3. sharp angles of her cheekbones
4. cheeks were wet with tears
5. high cheekbones
6. flat cheeks
7. thick cheeks
8. pronounced cheekbones
9. she had high, exotic cheekbones
10. tearstained cheeks
11. high strong cheekbones
12. a dusting of freckles on her cheeks
13. hollow of cheek

MT
MOUTH

MT1 MOUTH 1

MT2 MOUTH 2 (SHAPES - FULL)

1. mouth had gentle fullness
2. mouth was perfect
3. heavy mouth
4. he had a generous mouth
5. big sweet mouth
6. red, full-lipped mouth
7. large mouth

MT3 MOUTH 3 (SHAPES - AVERAGE)

1. Well-cut mouth
2. delicately shaped mouth

MT4 MOUTH 4 (SHAPES - THIN)

1. his mouth was thin with a cynical twist to it
2. hard, thin and disdainful

MT5 MOUTH 5 (OPEN)

1. openmouthed
2. the moistness of her open mouth
3. a slight yawn

MT6 MOUTH 6 (CLOSED)

1. clamped mouth
2. mouth was compressed
3. the rosette of her mouth the hard line of his mouth
4. mouth was tight and grim
5. down-turned mouth
6. pursed mouth
7. tight-mouthed
8. folded subtle mouth

MT7 MOUTH 7 (DRY)

1. mouth was parched and dry
2. dry mouth

MT8 MOUTH 8 (WET)

1. mouth was flecked with foam
2. the moistness of her open mouth
3. a fleck of saliva
4. moist, firm mouth
5. a trickle of saliva

MT9 MOUTH 9 (COLOR)

1. her mouth was a smiling rosy flower
2. mouth was as pale as her cheeks
3. her faintly rosy mouth

MT10 MOUTH 10 (LOCATIONS)

1. mouth corner
2. the roof of her mouth
3. inner-walls of her mouth
4. dark velvet recesses of her mouth
5. the walls of her mouth
6. recesses of her mouth
7. one corner of his mouth
8. the line of his mouth
9. into his mouth
10. over her mouth
11. the corners of her mouth turned upwards more than they turned down
12. there were touches of humor around the mouth
13. one hand to his mouth
14. taut lines between her nose and mouth

MT11 MOUTH 11 (NEGATIVE EXPRESSIONS)

1. a sympathetic frown

2. ironic sneer
3. a suspicious line at the corners of his mouth
4. mouth of contempt
5. a moue of distaste
6. the hard line of his mouth
7. mouth was tight and grim
8. melancholy frown
9. frowning heavily
10. cruel line of his mouth
11. a sullen thwarted pout
12. a mouth of contempt
13. his mouth was thin with a cynical twist to it
14. mouth is unhappily petulant
15. a signature pout
16. a sober frown

MT12 MOUTH 12 (POSITIVE EXPRESSION)

1. her mouth was a smiling rosy flower
2. she had a genial mouth
3. he had a humorous, kindly mouth
4. there were touches of humor around the mouth

MT13 MOUTH 13 (OTHER)

1. there were age lines about his mouth, muting his youth with
2. mouth was warm and demanding
3. the sweetness of her mouth
4. firm mouth
5. could feel the sour taste of vomit in her mouth
6. uncompromisingly cruel mouth
7. bright mouth
8. her heart in her mouth

LS

LIPS

LS1 LIPS 1

LS2 LIPS 2 (SHAPES - FULL)

1. full lips
2. the soft fullness of her lips
3. soft lips
4. pliant lips
5. her lips full land rounded over even teeth
6. full sensuous lips
7. lips like petals
8. red, full-lipped mouth
9. bruised grape-pulp lips
10. thick lips
11. full lower lip
12. kissable lips
13. lips were full
14. wide-lipped
15. labile lips

LS3 LIPS 3 (SHAPES - THIN)

1. compressed lips
2. long, thin lips

LS4 LIPS 4 (OPEN)

1. between slack lips
2. generously curved parted lips
3. lips looking as though they'd just been kissed
4. parted lips
5. pliant lips
6. wobbling lips
7. kissable lips

LS5 LIPS 5 (CLOSED)

1. a pouted lower lip
2. clamped lips
3. clasped lips
4. pursed lips
5. lips were pursed as if for a whistle
6. lips tightly compressed
7. lips were pressed together
8. compressed lips
9. pinched lips
10. pursed lips
11. a small close-lipped smile
12. tightlipped

LS6 LIPS 6 (WET)

1. lips looking as though they'd just been kissed
2. lips warm and moist
3. pliant lips
4. foam on his lips

LS7 LIPS 7 (DRY)

1. from between dry lips
2. on his lips
3. lips had gone dry

LS8 LIPS 8 (SOFT)

1. lips were like velvet
2. lips were warm and soft and firm

LS9 LIPS 9 (LOCATION)

1. a pouted lower lip
2. on her lips
3. across his lips
4. bottom lip
5. between his lips
6. around her lips
7. against her lips
8. between slack lips
9. an uncontrolled twitch of the lip
10. from between dry lips
11. lower lip
12. red under-lip
13. under-lip
14. full lower lip

LS10 LIPS 10 (NEGATIVE EXPRESSION)

1. demanding lips
2. a cute little grimace
3. grim-lipped

LS11 LIPS 11 (COLOR)

1. slightly tinted lips
2. smooth marble like lips
3. the blush of her lips
4. there was a soft color in her sweet curled lips
5. red under-lip
6. pale lips
7. bruised grape-pulp lips
8. red, full-lipped mouth
9. lips looking as though they'd just been kissed

LS12 LIPS 12 (OTHER)

1.   an uncontrolled twitch of the lip
2.   heavily mustached lips
3.   the touch of his lips
4.   lips were surprisingly soft and sensitive warm lips
5.   trembling lips
6.   strong hardness of his lips
7.   lips were warm and sweet
8.   sweet throbbing of his lips
9.   the pressure of his lips
10.   a trace of a smile on his lips
11.   curved lips
12.   salt on his lips
13.   kissable lips
14.   generously curved parted lips
15.   a small twitch of lip
16.   there was a soft color in her sweet curled lips
17.   temptingly curved mouth
18.   panting lips
19.   calm set of the withered lips
20.   wrinkled lips
21.   cracked and tender skin of his lips

SM
SMILES

SM1 SMILES 1

SM2 SMILES 2 (POSITIVE)

1.   tolerant smile
2.   an infectious smile
3.   boyishly affectionate smile

4. a slow steady smile of happiness
5. mercurial smile
6. the smile in his eyes
7. a small smile of enchantment
8. smile was eager and alive with affection and delight
9. the warm glow of his smile
10. disarming smile
11. smile was without malice
12. a, slow secret smile
13. forgiving smile
14. a depth to her smile
15. smile was magnetic
16. smile of thanks
17. an unconscious smile
18. his smile was as intimate as a kiss
19. leisurely smile
20. friendly smile
21. his smile had a spark of eroticism
22. thoughtful smile
23. captivating smile
24. smile was bright
25. beautiful candid smile
26. an easy smile
27. a superior smile
28. a smile that became her
29. comfortable smile
30. a quick smile
31. provocative smile
32. pleasant smile
33. understanding smile
34. smiled amiably
35. a hot, slow smile
36. good-natured smile
37. her smile was cheerful
38. a sad, fond smile
39. sensuous smile of pleasure

40. smile has light
41. wide-eyed smile
42. a shiny smile was the softest thing about her
43. comical smile
44. a smile of measured approval
45. warmest of smiles
46. a smile of sweet reason
47. a smile of radiant innocence
48. a bright and pretty smile
49. a happy glazed smile
50. openhearted smile
51. wonderful smile
52. an affectionate smile
53. her best asset was   her smile
54. a youthful smile
55. wide and delighted smile
56. a smile of great sweetness
57. an expression of suppressed mirth
58. beatific smile
59. a good smile
60. a fierce grin of joyous anticipation
61. a smile that went straight to his heart
62. a rich smile
63. a shooting star of a smile
64. lines of good humor on his mouth
65. a genuine smile

SM3 SMILES 3 (NEGATIVE)

1. slightly puzzled smile
2. a bitter grimace
3. cynical smile
4. cold grey of his watchful smile
5. a forced smile
6. a slow, secret smile
7. brittle smile

8.   satanic smile
9.   curved, stiff smile
10.   smile was without humor
11.   a slight smile of defiance
12.   a smile of nonchalance
13.   mocking smile
14.   bemused smile
15.   buttery smile
16.   a shadowy ironic sneer
17.   gloating smile
18.   a bleak smile
19.   a marvelously obscure and unrepentant smile
20.   a suggestion of a smirk
21.   half-hesitant smile
22.   a tight smile
23.   a small grimace
24.   a lordly smile
25.   a mocking smile
26.   a wintry smile
27.   a jovial smile fixed on his face
28.   a slow smile
29.   a smile of vapid bliss
30.   an entirely incongruous smile
31.   an over-bright smile
32.   mirthless smile
33.   wry smile
34.   a placating smirk
35.   a smile without humor
36.   a rather helpless smile
37.   a rather vindictive grin
38.   a smile of confusion
39.   a forced smile
40.   mad smile
41.   death-head grin
42.   a fierce grin of joyous anticipation
43.   smile held no joy

44. a weak smile
45. a superior smile
46. malevolent grin
47. a secret smile
48. a frightening grin
49. smile was tinged with horror
50. a hard smile
51. his smile was bland
52. a smile without mirth
53. an embarrassed smile

SM4 SMILES 4 (BIG)

1. a shooting star of a smile
2. mercurial smile
3. wide, open smile
4. a brilliant smile
5. wide and delighted smile
6. broad smile
7. a huge smile
8. his smile was wide
9. her most brilliant smile

SM5 SMILES 5 (SMALL)

1. a ghost of a smile
2. thin-lipped smile
3. small smile of enchantment
4. a small, shy smile
5. a bland half smile
6. demure smile
7. a wry smile
8. a tremulous smile
9. ghost of a smile

10. quirk of a smile
11. a trace of a smile
12. a private smile
13. a small, lost smile
14. trace of a smile
15. a small smile
16. a weak smile
17. shadow of a smile
18. a thin smile
19. a strange little smile
20. a glimmer of a smile
21. a shadow of a smile
22. a slight smile

SM6 SMILES 6 (LOCATION)

1. beneath the smile
2. her smile long-ranged but very visible

SM7 SMILES 7 (GRINS)

1. a sudden grin
2. irresistibly devastating grin
3. sour grin
4. wide grin
5. derisive grin
6. a boyish grin
7. grinning like demented idiots
8. weary grin
9. fatuous grin
10. a fierce grin of joyous anticipation
11. a frightening grin
12. twisted grin
13. grinning mouth

14. death-head grin
15. crooked grin
16. wry grin
17. an idiot grin
18. a rather vindictive grin

SM8 SMILES 8 (OTHER)

1. twisted smile
2. sudden smile
3. a certain smile
4. smile was noncommittal
5. wistful smile
6. a lewd smile
7. a smile of combined satisfaction and derision
8. tolerant smile

FR
FROWNS

FR1 FROWNS 1

1. a concentrated frown
2. a rueful grimace
3. a mock grimace of pain

KS
KISSES

KS1 KISSES 1

1. ceremonial kiss
2. taunting little kisses
3. kiss was surprisingly gentle
4. little soft kisses
5. kiss was slow, thoughtful

6. kiss was easy, practiced
7. velvet warmth of his kiss
8. kiss was as tender and light as a summer breeze
9. a light questioning kiss
10. a gentle drugging kiss
11. bruising kiss
12. punishing kiss
13. rough, aggressive kiss
14. kiss was as challenging as it was rewarding
15. a perfunctory kiss
16. taunting little kisses
17. one indelible kiss
18. kiss was white-hot
19. the explosion of his kiss
20. a kiss full of passion and need
21. wildly masculine sensation of his kiss
22. kiss was a soul-reaching massage
23. near kisses
24. slow, shivery kisses
25. a kiss for her tired soul
26. first kiss
27. wild, hungry kiss
28. a kiss that threatened to bruise her lips
29. warm kiss
30. gentle brush of her lips on
31. a smacking kiss on the cheek
32. slobbering kisses
33. little soft kisses
34. unexpectedly sensual kiss
35. gentle kiss

TN
TONGUE

TN1 TONGUE 1

TN2 TONGUE 2 (COLOR)

1. red rosette of her tongue

TN3 TONGUE 3 (UNHEALTHY)

1. swollen tongue
2. dry tongue
3. cracked tongue

TN4 TONGUE 4 (SPEECH)

1. rebel tongue
2. sharp tongue
3. tongue-tied veneration
4. sharp-tongued
5. liquid tongue
6. the word felt lumpy on his tongue
7. clicking tongue

TN5 TONGUE 5 (OTHER)

1. the flirt of her little tongue
2. her tongue was dry as dust
3. thrusting tongue
4. tongue-tip
5. point of her tongue
6. tip of her tongue
7. hot tongue
8. rough tongue of a steel rasp
9. dainty tongue

TH
TEETH

TH1 TEETH 1

TH2 TEETH 2 (GOOD)

1. her lips full and rounded over even teeth
2. dazzling display of straight, white teeth
3. the even whiteness of her smile
4. even teeth
5. perfect teeth
6. even and white teeth
7. sudden flash of white teeth
8. strikingly white teeth
9. good teeth

TH3 TEETH 3 (OTHER)

1. his chops

TH4 TEETH 4 (BAD)

1. Rat-like teeth
2. discolored tooth
3. dagger--like teeth
4. rotten teeth
5. teeth were stained
6. teeth were dirty
7. cruel yellow teeth
8. toothed

TH5 TEETH 5 (LOCATION)

1. between his teeth
2. smooth wetness of her teeth

VC

VOICE

VC1 VOICE 1

VC2 VOICE 2 (PLEASANT)

1. a resonant voice
2. voice was honeysweet
3. calming voice
4. her voice was well enunciated
5. a sensuous tone
6. voice was true, resonant, very nearly operatic quality
7. sweet virginal soprano voice
8. quiet, insistent voice
9. laconic voice
10. voice was little more than a whisper
11. unintelligible music of their speech
12. a deep voice
13. almost rolling voice
14. a cheery kind of voice
15. deep and gentle voice
16. magnificent ringing voice
17. small true voice
18. pretty voice
19. honey sweet voice
20. voice like low, soft music
21. a rich voice
22. a piping voice
23. a voice as musical as a harp
24. strangely clear voice
25. breathy voice

VC3 VOICE 3 (UNPLEASANT)

1. a thin voice
2. a stentorian voice
3. an extremely loud voice
4. piping little voice
5. a tiny whining shriek
6. a voice hoarse with nervousness
7. yells of fury
8. hollow whisper
9. a voice too low to overhear
10. raw grate of his voice
11. deep voice
12. cracking voice
13. thin sharp voice
14. wild scream of agony
15. a barely audible whisper
16. low trembly voice
17. distant voice
18. crackly voice
19. a tiny cough
20. a brazen voice
21. a scratchy voice
22. deep bass voice
23. deep voice which seemed bigger than he was
24. mincing voice
25. a syrupy voice
26. a deep hollow voice
27. bumbling voice
28. shaking voice
29. low urgent whisper
30. a grave note in her voice
31. a barely audible whisper
32. voice was thin to the cracking point
33. voice not quite in control
34. his voice cracked all to pieces as if someone had struck him in the chest
35. bawling with horror

36.   voice was a little pompous
37.   a twittering call
38.   dubious tone
39.   a hoarse croak
40.   cry was one of raw horror
41.   a squeak of protest
42.   voice held a ragged edge of hysteria
43.   a warning voice
44.   a caustic tone
45.   thin pathetic yells
46.   there was something in her voice that made him look up
47.   there was an edge to his voice
48.   her voice, shrill with impatience and ill-humor

VC4 VOICE 4 (DISTINCT ACCENTS)

1.   talking slightly down-East
2.   unusually gentle
3.   upper class accent
4.   soft, a smooth and subtle tongue
5.   voice had a curious exotic quality
6.   local tongue

VC5 VOICE 5 (NEUTRAL)

1.   his voice was carefully neutral
2.   voice was curiously flat
3.   a monotonous gentle tone that soothed the ears
4.   even monotone voice
5.   his voice was held at a neutral dead level
6.   voice was deadly polite
7.   subdued chatter

VC6 VOICE 6 (WHISPER)

1. a stage whisper, designed to be heard by everyone in the room

LH
LAUGHTER

LH1 LAUGHTER 1

LH2 LAUGHTER 2 (PLEASANT)

1. a fine breaker of laughter
2. a deep laugh
3. a little cry of pleasure

LH3 LAUGHTER 3 (UNPLEASANT)

1. a brittle laugh
2. a short laugh
3. a sorrowful laugh
4. a short bark of humor-lacking laughter
5. a shrill edged laugh
6. laugh was wild
7. high laughter
8. squalled with laughter
9. a little sneeze of laughter
10. a shrill cackling laugh not unlike screaming
11. his laugh was almost a giggle

LH4 LAUGHTER 4 (STRONG)

1. exultant laughter

CY
CRYING

CY1 CRYING 1

1. restless mewling cry of a hungry baby
2. another strangled sob

BG
BREATHING

BG1 BREATHING 1

BG2 BREATHING 2 (COMFORTABLY)

1. regular breathing of slumber
2. a deep inhale
3. a breath of satisfaction
4. a deep puff
5. a deep breath

BG3 BREATHING 3 (UNCOMFORTABLY)

1. sobbing breaths
2. harsh gasps
3. a gasping cry
4. breathless sobbing
5. a long shuddering breath
6. a hissing breath
7. a gusty sigh
8. breath-catching excitement
9. gasping breaths
10. rib-stretching gasps
11. heavy breathing close to a sob

BG4 BREATHING 4 (BREATH)

1. in mid-breath
2. under his breath

3.   her breath was fearsome
4.   intake of breath

CG
COUGHING

CG1 COUGHING 1

1. a tiny cough

JW
JAW

JAW 1

1. sharp jaw
2. long jaw
3. a hard jaw
4. narrow jaw
5. busted jaw
6. heavy jowled
7. outthrust jaw

CN
CHIN

CN1 CHIN 1

CN2 CHIN 2 (HAIRLESS)

1. smoothly barbered
2. clean-shaven

CN3 CHIN 3 (POINTED)

1. sharp, clear chin
2. pointed chin
3. cleft chin
4. strong chin
5. stubborn chin
6. round chin
7. determined and forceful chin

CN4 CHIN 4 (OTHER)

1. hands were raised toward his chin in the ancient attitude of prayer
2. soft sag beneath the chin
3. chin up
4. her chin cupped in her hands

NK
NECK

NK1 NECK 1

NK2 NECK 2 (LOCATION)

1. nape of the neck
2. juncture of the neck and clavicle
3. the hollow between his shoulder and neck
4. atop his neck

NK3 NECK 3 (OTHER)

1. poised neck
2. translucence of her neck
3. the creamy expanse of her neck

4. a pouched and flabby neck
5. a tendoned neck
6. cords in his neck

TR
THROAT

TR1 THROAT 1

TR2 THROAT 2 (LOCATION)

1. juncture of the jaw and throat
2. somewhere deep in the depths of her throat
3. beneath his throat
4. the creased skin of his throat
5. against his throat

TR3 THROAT 3 (OTHER)

1. throat was dry
2. a constricted throat
3. bruised throat

SH
SHOULDERS

SH1 SHOULDERS 1

SH2 SHOULDERS 2 (BIG)

1. mostly shoulders
2. broad shouldered
3. broad shoulders
4. wide shouldered

5. wide shoulders
6. huge shoulders
7. square shouldered
8. wide shoulders

SH3 SHOULDERS 3 (STRAIGHT - STRONG)

1. neat shoulders
2. sharp line of his shoulders
3. wide shouldered
4. well-muscled shoulders
5. huge shoulders
6. the powerful set of shoulders
7. muscle humped shoulders
8. square shouldered
9. a supporting shoulder

SH4 SHOULDERS 4 (BENT - WEAK)

1. rounded shoulders
2. hunched shoulders
3. shoulders were bowed
4. stoop-shouldered

SH5 SHOULDERS 5 (LOCATIONS)

1. across his shoulder
2. head thrust forward on wide shoulders
    3. the hollow between his shoulder and neck
4. against his shoulder
5. over her shoulder
6. sharp line of his shoulders
7. a supporting shoulder

SH6 SHOULDERS 6 (EXPRESSIONS - NEGATIVE)

1. a strange shrug
2. a helpless shrug
3. an impatient shrug
4. an owlish shrug
5. a bored shrug

SH7 SHOULDERS 7 (EXPRESSIONS - POSITIVE)

1. Shoulder-shrugging grace

SH8 SHOULDERS 8 (OTHER)

1. naked shoulders
2. head thrust forward on wide shoulders
3. her shoulders smooth
4. bare skin of her shoulders

SH9 SHOULDERS 9 (BLADES)

1. sharp shoulder blades

<u>CS</u>
<u>CHEST</u>

CS1 CHEST 1

CS2 CHEST 2 (LARGE)

1. enormous chest
2. broad chest

3. barrel chest
4. deep-chested
5. huge chest
6. pigeon-chested

CS3 CHEST 3 (SMALL)

1. emaciated chest

CS4 CHEST 4 (HAIRLESS)

1. hairless chest

CS5 CHEST 5 (HAIRY)

1. chest as furry as a monkey

CS6 CHEST 6 (LOCATION)

1. his chest quite high
2. across his chest
3. close to his chest
4. against his chest

CS7 CHEST 7 (OTHER)

1. aching chest
2. corded muscles of his chest

RB
RIBS

RB1 RIBS 1

---

1. lower ribs
2. small ribs

BS
BREAST

BS1 BREAST 1

BS2 BREAST 2 (LARGE)

1. her stern was hefty, shapely
2. big breasts
3. her breasts were high and full
4. pert, rounded breasts, remarkable in size
5. big-breasted
6. bosomy

BS3 BREAST 3 (FIRM)

1. out-thrust breasts
2. sassily up-tilted breasts
3. pert, rounded breasts, remarkable in size
4. her stern was hefty, shapely
5. her breasts were high and full
6. splendid wheels
7. her breasts were full and tight, laced with blue veins
8. her breasts, outlined beneath the low-buttoned blouse, seemed more prominent than usual

BS4 BREAST 4 (LOCATION)

1. breast level

BS5 BREAST 5 (CLEAVAGE)

1.   a glimpse of cleavage

BS6 BREAST 6 (NIPPLES)

1.   pert nipples

BS7 BREAST 7 (OTHER)

1.   Half-naked breast
2.   promise of her breasts
3.   splendid wheels
4.   her breasts were full and tight, laced with blue veins
5.   vicious marks on her breasts

HT
HEART

HT1 HEART 1

1.   a sore and jealous heart
2.   rushing heart
3.   fast-beating heart
4.   pumping heart
5.   her heart in her mouth

BL
BELLY

BL1 BELLY 1

BL2 BELLY 2 (FLAT)

1. flat belly

BL3 BELLY 3 (FAT)

1. protruding potbelly
2. thickened with childbearing
3. folds of his belly

BL4 BELLY 4 (OTHER)

1. hollow of her navel
2. his heaving middle

WT

WAIST

WT1 WAIST 1

WT2 WAIST 2 (THIN)

1. slender waist
2. thin waist

WT3 WAIST 3 (LOCATION)

1. bare to the waist

WT4 WAIST 4 (GESTURES)

1. a courtly bow
2. a ceremonious little bow
3. a courteous bow

4. a low bow
5. her bow was almost perfunctory
6. a curt bow

WT5 WAIST 5 (OTHER)

1. bare to the waist

WT6 WAIST 6 (SIDES)

1. on his side
BK
BACK

BK1 BACK 1

BK2 BACK 2 (STRAIGHT)

1. arrow straight
2. rigid as a sleepwalker
3. straight back

BK3 BACK 3 (BENT)

1. bowed back

BK4 BACK 4 (LOCATION)

1. small of his back
2. Muscles of his back
3. a crick in his back
4. behind him

BK5 BACK 5 (OTHER)

1. muscles of his back
2. a crick in his back

BT
BUTTOCKS

BT1 BUTTOCKS 1

BT2 BUTTOCKS 2 (ROUNDED)

1. firm curve of her buttocks
2. sex of the curves
3. the gentle curve of her full buttocks
4. curve of her buttocks

BT3 BUTTOCKS 3 (OTHER)

1. haunches
2. from behind, she looked her age

HP
HIPS

HP1 HIPS 1

HP2 HIPS 2 (NARROW)

1. slim hips

HP3 HIPS 3 (WIDE)

1. flared hips
HP4 HIPS 4 (LOCATION)

1. hands on hips

HP5 HIPS 5 (OTHER)

1. a fine hip-swing

AR
ARMS

AR1 ARMS 1

AR2 ARMS 2 (LARGE)

1. Thick-armed and agile
2. beefy arms
3. club-like forearm
4. forearms like clubs
5. arm like an oak

AR3 ARMS 3 (SMALL)

1. his arms looked like they had been squeezed from tubes

AR4 ARMS 4 (LONG)

1. long arm
2. his arms looked like they had been squeezed from tubes

AR5 ARMS 5 (STRONG)

1. muscular arms
2. arm like an oak
3. forearms like clubs
4. club-like forearm
5. supporting arm

AR6 ARMS 6 (WEAK)

1.   his arms seemed to be as boneless as tentacles

AR7 ARMS 7 (GESTURES)

1.   an extravagant gesture
2.   folded arms

AR8 ARMS 8 (LOCATIONS)

1.   forearm
2.   the hollow of his arm

AR9 ARMS 9 (OTHER)

1.   a ready arm
2.   friendly arms
3.   sheltering arms, tender embrace
4.   outstretched arms

AP1 ARMPITS 1 (OTHER)

1.   shaven armpits

EB
ELBOW

EB1 ELBOW 1 (LOCATION)

1.   in the bend of her elbow
2.   the hollow of his arm

HN
HANDS

HN1 HANDS 1 (BIG)

1. a ham-like fist
2. big hands
3. a hand like a side of meat
4. large hands
5. big hands
6. two hands that would cover a coffee table

HN2 HANDS 2 (SMALL)

1. slender white hands
2. skeleton thin hand
3. narrow hand
4. fine boned hand

HN3 HANDS 3 (STRONG)

1. a tight grip
2. frail strength in her hand
3. prisoning hand
4. a firm grip
5. restraining hand

HN4 HANDS 4 (WEAK)

1. slack hand
2. trembling hands
3. hands were damply flaccid

HN5 HANDS 5 (LOCATION)

1. in cupped hands
2. open palm

3. balled fists
4. openhanded
5. with the back of his hand
6. the back of his hand
7. arms at her sides
8. the back of his hand
9. the flat of his hand
10. hands on hips
11. a handful
12. outstretched hands
13. flat of the hand
14. with one hand
15. with the fingers of both hands

HN6 HANDS 6 (GESTURES)

1. wide gesture
2. friendly handshake
3. nervous gesture
4. free hand had become a fist
5. a graceful gesture
6. a grip of rough affection
7. little intimate touches of the hand
8. furious gesture
9. a polite gesture of restraint
10. a pretty, half-deprecating gesture
11. folded hands
12. a salute of upraised palms
13. hands look serene
14. outstretched appealing hands
15. a casual gesture
16. a graceful gesture
17. outstretched hands
18. derisive gestures
19. a friendly, upraised palm
20. a touching gesture

21. an unpracticed gesture
22. clenched fists
23. lively hands
24. a wild gesture
25. her hands were flutteringly busy
26. swift gesture
27. the offered hand

HN7 HANDS 7 (HAIRY)

1. great hairy hands

HN8 HANDS 8 (OTHER)

1. Empty-handed
2. eager hands
3. restless hands
4. a lazy hand
5. bloodied hand
6. leathery hand
7. slippery hands
8. fond slap
9. shaking hands
10. attempted caress
11. suddenly damp palms
12. gentle hand
13. the touch of his hand
14. moist hands
15. tapping hand
16. gentle touch
17. hands were stiff

HN9 HANDS 9 (PALMS - LOCATION)

1. open palm

2. in her palm
3. open palm of his hand
4. the flat of his hand
5. heel of one hand over the other
6. a friendly, upraised palm
7. palms spread flat

HN10 HANDS 10 (PALMS - OTHER)

1. blistered palms
2. the palms of her hands were damp
3. pale-palmed hand
4. betrayingly damp palms

WR
WRIST

WR1 WRIST 1

1. through her wrists

FN
FINGERS

FN1 FINGERS 1

FN2 FINGERS 2 (LARGE)

1. thick finger
2. ham forefinger
3. thick fingered
4. horny fingers
5. plump forefinger

FN3 FINGERS 3 (SMALL)

---

1. skinny little fingers like pincers

FN4 FINGERS 4 (LONG)

1. long fingers
2. long, slender fingers meant for plucking the strings of a lute

FN5 FINGERS 5 (SHORT)

1. a blunt finger

FN6 FINGERS 6 (STRONG)

1. strong fingers
2. firm fingers

FN7 FINGERS 7 (WEAK)

1. fumbling fingers
2. shaking fingers
3. palsied fingers
4. limp fingers
5. numbed fingers

FN8 FINGERS 8 (GESTURES)

1. pointed in a superfluous gesture
2. an upraised finger
3. bunched up fingers
4. pointing finger
5. a thumbs-up sign

6. the finger of ridicule
7. admonitory finger
8. crossed fingers
9. he pantomimed
10. with a cautious fingertip
11. tapping fingers

FN9 FINGERS 9 (LOCATIONS)

1. light finger tips
2. the tips of his fingers
3. with his thumb
4. with her little finger
5. on the top of one finger
6. on the pads of the finger
7. loosely between his fingers
8. fingers interlocked
9. crossed fingers
10. a fingertip touch
11. finger ends
12. fingers tight lying one to another
13. with the fingers of both hands
14. tip of his thumb
15. tip of forefinger
16. with a cautious fingertip

FN10 FINGERS 10 (OTHER)

1. a finger's breadth
2. with great tender fingers
3. loving fingers bunched up fingers
4. a thumbs-up sign
5. an exploratory finger   callused fingers
6. cool, impersonal fingers
7. knotted fingers

8. tense fingers
9. sticky fingers
10. a grazed finger
11. cool fingers
12. the finger of ridicule
13. nimble fingers

FN11 FINGERS 11 (KNUCKLES - LOCATION)

1. knuckle to lip
2. the backs of his knuckles
3. the knuckle of his forehand

FN12 FINGERS 12 (KNUCKLES - OTHER)

1. knuckles were white with tension
2. joints of her fingers were swollen and reddened
3. across one knuckle
4. knuckles stood out as pale knobs
5. whitened knuckles

FN13 FINGERS 13 (NAILS)

1.   Claw-like fingernails
2.   all around the fingernails
3.   the nails of her hand
4.   a neatly manicured finger
5.   nails were badly broken
6.   clean nails
7.   nails like talons
8.   neat nails
9.   trimmed nails
10.   overgrown nails
11.   beneath her nails

LG
LEGS

LG1 LEGS 1

LG2 LEGS 2 (LONG)

1.   long slim legs
2.   long, bare legs
3.   long-stemmed
4.   long legs

LG3 LEGS 3 (SHORT)

1.   diminutive legs

LG4 LEGS 4 (ATTRACTIVE)

1.   long slim legs
2.   legs were quite stunning
3.   awesome legs
4.   very nice legs
5. wonderful legs

LG5 LEGS 5 (UNATTRACTIVE)

1. legs were withered and loose-veined

LG6 LEGS 6 (SKINNY)

1. skinny legs
2. stick legs

LG7 LEGS 7 (STRONG)

1.   strong legs

LG8 LEGS 8 (HAIRY)

1.   legs lightly dusted with golden hair

LG9 LEGS 9 (BARE)

1.   shaven legs
2.   long, bare legs

LG10 LEGS 10 (LOCATION)

1.   Cross-legged
2.   legs straight out from
3.   legs resting on
4.   crossed at the ankle
5.   her lap

LG11 LEGS 11 (OTHER)

1.   brisk walk
2.   a nervous pace
3.   legs were stiff
4.   a noiseless woods walk
5.   in a single leap
6.   a hard scramble up
7.   snakes progress
8.   a loping run
9.   arrogant stride
10.   confident stride
11.   a series of hops
12.   languid carriage

13.   restless pacing
14.   slow steps
15.   stately, slow-motion gait
16.   authoritative stride
17.   a small curtsey

LG12 LEGS 12 (THIGHS)

1.   thews like an oak
2.   between her thighs
3.   her inner thigh
4.   exposed length of lightly tanned thigh
5.   long, straight thighs
6.   a strange ache in the thigh muscles
7.   a swing of rhythmic poetry in her strong thighs

LG13 LEGS 13 (KNEES - LOCATION)

1.   on his knees
2.   to his knees
3.   across his knees
4.   down on one knee

LG14 LEGS 14 (KNEES - OTHER)

1.   hunched knees
2.   bent knees

LG15 LEGS 15 (CALVES - LOCATION)

1.   fell to mid calf
2.   inner surface of the calf

LG16 LEGS 16 (CALVES - OTHER)

1.   trim shanks
2.   bowlegged

LG17 LEGS 17 (ANKLES - LOCATION)

1.   around her ankle

LG18 LEGS 18 (ANKLES - OTHER)

1.   a sprained ankle
2.   a lot of ankle exposed
3.   strong ankles

FE
FEET

FE1 FEET 1

FE2 FEET 2 (BIG)

1.   swollen feet

FE3 FEET 3 (SMALL)

1.   feet were small
2.   diminutive feet
3.   slim feet

FE4 FEET 4 (PRETTY)

1.   finely shaped feet

FE5 FEET 5 (UGLY)

1.   swollen feet

FE6 FEET 6 (LOCATION)

1.   beneath the soles of her feet
2.   feet widespread
3.   her feet up
4.   stood, feet apart
5.   feet first
6.   along her instep
7.   was half on his feet
8.   soles of feet

FE7 FEET 7 (OTHER)

1.   quick footsteps
2.   firm footing
3.   flat feet
4.   silent feet
5.   rested his weight on his heels
6.   step was sure and confident
7.   an almost soundless footfall
8.   light on her feet
9.   fog-footed
10.   stockinged feet
11.   barefoot
12.   surefooted

FE8 FEET 8 (TOES - LOCATION)

1.   under her toes
2.   on tiptoe

FE9 FEET 9 (TOES - OTHER)

1.   long narrow toes

BY
BODY

BY1 BODY 1

BY2 BODY 2 (MUSCLES)

1. awesomely muscled
2. built like a sumo wrestler
3. strength that seemed to rival that of a stallion
4. tense cords of muscle
5. even his shoulders were muscled
6. every muscle was tense
7. muscles bulged and slid
8. cramped muscles
9. taut muscle over hard, compact bone
10. muscular bulk
11. hard body
12. Mr. Body-perfect
13. every tendon taut
14. stiff muscles
15. a built-for-action body
16. slim but powerfully built
17. corded muscles
18. a heavy peasant's body, sturdy and hard, bursting with juice
19. glistening muscles, hard, distinct
20. bulging muscles

BY3 BODY 3 (BONES)

1. taut muscle over hard, compact bone
2. creeping chill in his bones

BY4 BODY 4 (FRAME - LARGE)

1. a bull of a man
2. a giant of a man
3. a fine mountain of a man
4. a majestic figure
5. big frame
6. a great husky man
7. he was built like a beer wagon
8. a heavy peasant's body, sturdy and hard, bursting with juice

BY5 BODY 5 (FRAME - SMALL)

1. a vigorous, elfin man
2. a wiry hawk-like man
3. skeleton thin
4. as neatly packaged and self-contained as an egg
5. a tight-knot man
6. he looked like a little wet bird
7. the tiny, frail body

BY6 BODY 6 (WEIGHT - HEAVY)

1. a bull of a man
2. ponderous mass of flesh
3. obscene in it's obesity
4. a heavy peasant's body, sturdy and hard, bursting with juice
5. soft with fat
6. a great husky man
7. a fine mountain of a man
8. pudgy figure
9. a short, plump polyp of a man
10. chubby
11. an obese, sloppy man
12. a good hefty body
13. he was built like a beer wagon

BY7 BODY 7 (WEIGHT - LIGHT)

1. lath thin body
2. painfully thin
3. a stately slim figure
4. so slight he could have snapped her in half with one blow of his enormous fist
5. lissome slenderness
6. skeleton thin
7. long lean form
8. lean body
9. lithe as a snake
10. tall and straight, lithe and supple
11. a vigorous, elfin man
12. slender but voluptuous body
13. sword-thin
14. slim but powerfully built
15. the tiny, frail body

BY8 BODY 8 (HEIGHT - TALL)

1. he towered above them like a mountain
2. tall, spare figure
3. tall, lanky frame
4. head and shoulders taller than most
5. rangy figure
6. she was tall, taller than average
7. a tall, willowy girl
8. tall and straight, lithe and supple
9. a majestic figure
10. a fine mountain of a man
11. on the tall side of six feet
12. a giant of a man

13. tall and rangy-rugged
14. a tall distinguished-looking man
15. she was a tall, sensual, animal
16. tall, athletic physique

BY9 BODY 9 (HEIGHT - AVERAGE)

1. she wasn't tall but she held herself like a queen

BY10 BODY 10 (HEIGHT - SHORT)

1. a vigorous, elfin man
2. a man of slight stature and even slighter hair
3. a short man of stocky build
4. a short, plump polyp of a man

BY11 BODY 11 (AESTHETICS - POSITIVE)

1. arresting good looks
2. the picture of feminine certainty
3. lush torso
4. quite nicely proportioned
5. a lush, well formed body
6. nymphly figure
7. a pretty figure of a woman
8. his compelling personage
9. a heavy peasant's body, sturdy and hard, bursting with juice
10. the sensuality of his physique
11. his powerful presence
12. her body was sensuous
13. seductive, young body
14. a tall distinguished-looking man
15. a fine mountain of a man
16. trained body

17.   ripe-bodied
18.   she wasn't tall but she held herself like a queen
19.   tempting attractive male physique
20.   Mr. Body-perfect
21.   a barbaric figure
22.   she was a tall, sensual, animal
23.   tall, athletic physique
24.   a majestic figure
25.   her body that only weeks before had been swollen and misshapen
26.   slimmed back, with the resilience of youth, to a lithe tautness

BY12 BODY 12 (AESTHETICS - NEGATIVE)

1.   a barbaric figure
2.   body was stooped and ugly
3.   a short, plump polyp of a man
4.   he looked like the torpedo had already left the tube
5.   his body was shaped like a thimble
6.   an obese, sloppy man
7.   a physical monument to the terminal quality of youth
8.   he looked like a little wet bird
9.   there was something awkward and milk fed about him, like a calf

BY13 BODY 13 (POSTURES)
1.   every detail of his body showed as clearly as in death
2.   full-length on his back
3.   straight-backed stance of a knight
4.   the slouch of a frequenter of taverns
5.   a figure of fun
6.   a pose of defiance
7.   an attitude of frozen stillness
8.   she wasn't tall but she held herself like a queen

BY14 BODY 14 (HEALTHY)

PHYSICAL ATTRIBUTES
"DESCRIBING HUMAN ANATOMY"
INDEX

HEAD

FACE

HAIR

EARS

NOSE

CHEEKS

MOUTH

LIPS

SMILES

FROWNS

FEET

BODY

* In this book, you might notice several sections are very slim. I thought about removing those headings but left them purposely to help jog your thought processes. *

A note from Sybrina:

Once upon a time I wanted to be a writer more than anything in the world. I could tell stories with the best of them, so I just knew I could write well, too.

Funny thing about writing, though...it's nothing like telling a story. I bet you've noticed that, too. I'd even go as far as to bet there have been times...plenty of them, when you've been writing along just fine, then suddenly, you hit a brick wall over how to describe the simplest thing.

25 years ago, there wasn't anything much available other than Webster's Dictionary or Roget's Thesaurus and a couple of synonym and antonym books. So, I decided I'd start to put together what I was looking for, myself.

Those were the prehistoric days, before p.c.'s. Each bit of information I gathered was tediously placed behind index tabs in spiral notebooks...lots of notebooks and tons of tabs. It very quickly became a monstrous task. When I got my first computer, with Word Perfect's word "search and replace" features, I felt like I'd finally arrived in the 20th century but the best was yet to come. Word for Windows made cross-referencing all those phrases to all of their relevant categories a breeze.

Compiling this book has been a labor of love. Along the way, I have discovered my true writing skills lie, not in writing out my stories, but in organizing and categorizing information. Maybe someday, I'll actually have time to write my own great novel, but for now, I'm content in the knowledge that my work on Sybrina's Phrase Thesaurus has made it easier for other writers to get past their own brick walls. I hope you will enjoy reading the phrases in this tool as much as I have enjoyed compiling them.

Happy Writing! Visit www.sybrina.com to see other offerings.

Sybrina's Phrase
Thesaurus Series

Volume 1
Moving Parts – Part 1

Volume 2
Moving Parts – Part 2

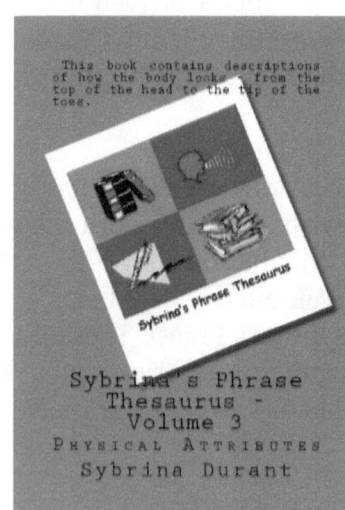

Volume 3
Physical Attributes

Volume 4
Earth Views

www.ingramcontent.com/pod-product-compliance
Lightning Source LLC
Chambersburg PA
CBHW020529290526
45786CB00002B/802